The Book of
PETER TAVY
with Cudlipptown

The Book of
PETER TAVY
with Cudlipptown

Two Coats Colder Than Tavistock

PETER TAVY HERITAGE GROUP

HALSGROVE

First published in Great Britain in 2002

Frontispiece photograph: *Watercolour of St Peter's Church, Peter Tavy, 1847, by an unknown artist.*

British Library Cataloguing-in-Publication Data
A CIP record for this title is available from the British Library

ISBN 1 84114 143 7

HALSGROVE

Halsgrove House
Lower Moor Way
Tiverton, Devon EX16 6SS
Tel: 01884 243242
Fax: 01884 243325
email: sales@halsgrove.com
website: www.halsgrove.com

Printed and bound by
Bookcraft Ltd, Midsomer Norton

Dedication

In the last year, since the start of this project, Peter Tavy has lost several of its older residents. Some were born and lived their whole lives in the village; others came on marriage and brought up their children here. To them, and all those who have helped to shape this parish in past years, we record our grateful thanks.

'For the children, the future builders of the mighty Empire.'
This photograph is thought to have been taken on 'Empire Day', 1902.

CONTENTS

Aerial view of the village of Peter Tavy, 2000.

ACKNOWLEDGEMENTS

It would be impossible to thank the legions of people, past and present, who have contributed to this volume. That it exists at all is a tribute to their interest in the people around them and the events they troubled to record, some in photographs, some in writing, but most often in the form of the memories they have carried with them over the years. Amongst those we list here who are due our grateful thanks should be included those who, with a single comment, enabled us to date an event or resolve a problem. We have used the tools of the internet and e-mail to collect history and memories from all over the world and it has never ceased to surprise us just how specially the families with roots in Peter Tavy still regard the village.

There will be many people to whom we have spoken whose names will not appear below; they are not forgotten and our thanks extend to them. Our grateful acknowledgements include: Eileen and Cyril Abel, Joan Amos, Sue Ellen Ash, Jane and Ken Ball, Arthur Bellamy, Enid and Bill Bellamy, Jessie Bellamy, Alison Bullock, Barbara Butterfield, Ann and Annie Cole, Frank and Ann Collins, John and Angela Collins, Jean Course, Kathy Crantz, Ron Cubitt, Molly Cummings, Clara Davey, Phyllis and Ivy Dodd, Edward and Sandra Dodd, Jill and Jerry Morris, Eileen Duncan, Robin Fenner, Richard Friend, Betty Gilbert, Shirley Gill, Roger Grimley, Pauline Hamilton-Leggett, Valerie Hill, Joan Jeeves, Elsie Jeffery, John Kempe, Sher Leetooze, Jan Lightfoot, Michael Mates, Dorothy Maunder, Rachel Mudge, Norman Nankivell, James Perkins, Alec Phillott, Don Parker, Michael Rice, Barbara Schenck, Randolph and Kathleen Simmons, Marjorie and Dawn Sherrell, Liz Slack, Peggy Stephens, Peter and Pearl Tinson, Martin and Mary Wheddon, Betty Wilton, May Wakeham, Mary Warne, Rob Weeks, Dorothy Williams and Gerald Williamson.

The Pony Drift, 1975. Left to right, back row: *Michael Bee, Jack Roskilly, Fred King, Cyril Abel;*
front row: *John Cole and Charles Mudge.*

Village Cross. The re-erection of the Village Cross after a century and a half was a part of the celebrations for the millennium 2000. The cross was taken down in the 1840s to make way for the horse-drawn hearses to turn at the church gate. Before this time families had carried the coffin to the church. Although the shaft and cross had been lost over the years, the base had been left lying at the side of the gate, and the mortice stone incorporated into the churchyard wall. The cross keys of St Peter cut into the stone by a medieval mason can be readily seen in the left panel of the mortice stone. Two fish, a Ram's head, a salamander, an anchor and an unidentified figure, possibly a rampant lion, can be seen in panels on the other sides.

INTRODUCTION

This is a book about a parish, a village, some small hamlets and the lives of the people who have lived here over the past 200 years. It is not the definitive history of this area. Inevitably we have strayed into earlier centuries because they have fashioned the lives of generations. No great families made their homes here and from early times freehold landowners have held the land alongside the Dukes of Cornwall and Bedford, the Radcliffes, the Hamlyns, the Bullers and the Tremaynes.

The task we set ourselves was to try to record some parts of the lives and work of the 'ordinary' people who make up the majority of the population; their work, their play and in particular their memories of Peter Tavy. A group which had formed to make a photographic survey of the parish for the millennium celebrations was approached and I agreed to coordinate our efforts. For several years I have been noting the reminiscences of those who lived in the village, and, through the medium of the internet, of people from all parts of the world. There was already a large archive in existence, resulting from the work done for Village Hall exhibitions going back to the early 1960s, and our thanks go to Michael Guest, Ray Downton and Peter Cox for a great deal of that work. It needed to be sorted and catalogued, a task not yet fully achieved as much of the material had to be put aside for the purposes of this book, as it is not readily reproduced. Valuable as contemporary newspaper reports can be, without a date they are difficult to place and many of the photographs are copies of copies, now scarcely fit to copy once again!

If there is one thing I have learnt, and should have learnt long ago, it is the need to date material and constantly check, re-check and check again the stories and memories of those kind enough to talk or write to me. Time is a great variable and what was yesterday to some is a year ago to others. We all know the problem!

In preparing the text I have been helped immensely by Donna Baker, Janet Bedford, Steve Carreck, Patrick Cashell and Angela Larcombe, each of whom has contributed to the book. I record my sincere thanks to them; however, I must accept for them, and for my own work, responsibility for errors of commission and omission. Apart from their own knowledge and memories of the village, to a greater or lesser extent they were working with information I had gleaned from the Devon County Record Office at Exeter and the City of Plymouth Office at Plymouth, as well as local sources. My sincere thanks must go to the archivists at both centres. My thanks also extend to Peter Jackman, who did much of the original scanning of photographs that have now gone out of our reach, and finally but as sincerely to all those who gave up their time to talk to me and help me understand the ways of the village and parish of Peter Tavy with Cudlipptown.

Roger Meyrick

Strip cultivation. The narrow strips of land still visible in fields above Godsworthy where villagers cultivated food for their families. Well into the nineteenth century, agricultural labourers might have had part of their wages paid in the form of access to a piece of land, plus annual amounts of dung or other dressing.

Tin workings above Wedlake. The watercourses with the rock and spoil thrown each side give some idea of the immense physical effort that must have been required before the days of heavy moving equipment (see also page 15).

A hut circle. One of many hut circles to be found in the early settlements above Willsworthy and elsewhere on the moor around Peter Tavy.

A BRIEF HISTORY

The village of Peter Tavy nestles into the western borders of Dartmoor some three miles north of Tavistock. Earlier known as Tavi Ffoliot or Petris Tavy, the parish can trace its origins into prehistory, when the Bronze-Age and Neolithic settlements to be found at Wedlake, White Tor, above Willsworthy, Standon and elsewhere were bustling villages in their own right.

The prehistoric trackway from the South Coast into the moor lay on the east of the river, crossing the Walkham at Horrabridge and the Tavy at Harford Bridge, before driving west to the Tamar and north to Okehampton. Before the abbey at Tavistock was founded, the site on which it was built was the 'stoc' or summer pasture of the Towi or Tavi settlement, thus giving the abbey the name of Tavistock. Now as then Peter Tavy is the natural gateway to the moor on the east of the River Tavy, a place where farmers, miners and traders have gathered for generations. It is described in the Domesday Book (1086) as:

... paying tax for one Hide. Land for 7 ploughs. In lordship 2 ploughs; 9 slaves; 5 villagers and 6 smallholders with 2 ploughs. Meadow 4 acres; pasture 16 furlongs long and 9 furlongs wide; woodland 3 furlongs long and 1 furlong wide; underwood 16 acres.

Dartmoor was affected by the plague, pestilence, famine and wars of the twelfth and early-thirteenth centuries after a period when the moors had been deserted and people had retired to the coast, or at least the valleys, during the climate changes of earlier centuries. From the appointment of Robert, chaplain of Tavy, to the church in around 1185, we hear nothing until Roger de Okeston is presented by the Priory at Plympton in 1270, when many people had moved back on to the moors, seeking a living from tin streaming and farming. Peter Tavy lay directly in line for such incursions.

The parish today is one of the largest in the county, extending from Harford Bridge on the east of the Tavy, though claiming half the river rights, to Hillbridge where it crosses the river to continue as far as Beardon, turning east and passing north of Willsworthy Common to Watern Oak and the source of the Tavy, where the boundary turns south to meet the Walkham river. Here it follows the river until turning west below Roos Tor and Staple Tor, but above Merrivale. Finally it makes its way back via Collaton Lane to Moorshop and the old Tavistock road to return to Harford Bridge west of Pitts Cleave. When the 'bounds were beaten' for the millennium it was calculated to be some 35 miles around the boundary, enclosing over 15 square miles (3,900 hectares).

In Saxon times, around 1042, Siward held the land of the manor of Petris Towi from the king, but following the Norman invasion it was awarded to Alfred the Breton, who also gained, amongst others in Devon, the manors of Huntingdon and Willsworthy that were to form the original parish. By the year 1200 the Ffoliot family had taken over and the village went by the name of Tavi Ffoliot. This was not to last long before it came into the hands of Ralph de Gorges who granted it to Rolf de Satchville. Now known as Taviton Petri, the greater part of the land passed to Adam de Brankescombe who sold much of it off to five freehold landowners with names that still ring an echo throughout Devon – Richard Jule, Roger Eleford, Roger Cole, Philip Babcombe and Walter Richard. It was only the markedly reduced manors of Peter Tavy and Huntingdon, with their related lordships, that were then given to the Abbey of Tavistock and subsequently passed into the hands of the Russell family, Dukes of Bedford, after the Reformation in 1539. More than 350 years later the Duke of Bedford, after some minor sales in the 1890s, finally sold his remaining cottages and land at auction in 1911.

Venville rents should be mentioned as being peculiar to those 28 parishes of which Peter Tavy is one, which have a border on the 'Forest or Chase of Dartmoor'. The rights available to the villagers of these parishes were of considerable significance since they could, by payment of the 'fine', not only turn their cattle on to the moor by day, though they had to be cleared by night unless a further 'fine' was paid, but also in 1382, they could 'have coals, turf, heath, furze, and stones for their own use', and in 1608:

... have in the Forrest of Dartmore all that maye doo hym good excepte grene ocke and venison, and if any of the said tenants shall have more catell than they maye winter apon his teneure, for to paye, for every oxe, cowe, and heaffer jd and every mare, horse and gelding ijd.

That there was poverty in Peter Tavy is certain, but with these opportunities available and traditional family responsibilities accepted, it was quite a few years before the word 'pauper' appeared in the parish churchwardens' accounts.

The successive Dukes of Bedford, through their stewards, maintained their rights and accepted their responsibilities as lords of the manors of Peter Tavy and Huntingdon. Courts Baron and Courts Leet were held regularly and dues and rents with 'frankpledge' were honoured. 'Frankpledge' was the system by which tenants would have responsibility for each other's good behaviour and answer to the courts for any failure. The last Court Leet to be held in Peter Tavy was in 1927.

Many of the settlements around Peter Tavy were fully established before the Domesday Book was drawn up in 1086. The manor of Peter Tavy was supported by the lordship with his villeins and six smallholders, men free to hold their own land so long as they gave service or taxes to their lord. Willsworthy Manor, held by Alfred the Breton after the Norman Conquest, was small with only a single virgate (approximately 30 acres) of land and four ploughs, with the lord of the manor holding land for one plough. There were 12 acres of woodland with pasture two leagues long (approximately six miles) by one league wide. The manor of Huntingdon, owned by the Abbey of Tavistock, was a submanor of Hurdwick that included the lands of Harragrove, Higher Churchtown, Tortown, Collaton, Wapsworthy, Coppithorne and Burgess Park, as well as Huntingdon itself, and there were a lot of individual fields such as Tiddyhawke, Pity, West Meadow and Gratten. The Huntingdon Manor Courts had been amalgamated with those of Peter Tavy by 1820 and the farm itself has since disappeared.

Cudlipptown, an even smaller manor, appears as Culitone in Domesday, with no more than the manor house and demesne farm, then called Butterworthy and identified as Butterberry today.

Within the next 300 years the whole parish of Peter Tavy became studded with farms. Radge, by 1180, and Nutley, already in Domesday, though strictly not within the parish but in Tavistock itself, together with Kingford, were among the earliest farms. Bowran, a family at Cox Tor in 1216, paid a fine to take up the tenancy, but the original buildings may well pre-date this by several hundred years. Wapsworthy by 1230, and Twist (otherwise called Twyste) by 1350 were well established, but Langsford in 1325 may pre-date these records as the name is derived from Langskaryford, an Anglo-Saxon word meaning 'the most distant point'. Sowtontown, then known as South Town, belongs to the same period being owned in 1361 by Richard Page, an early Member of Parliament for Tavistock. Gnattor (Nattor), where the Reep family later lived for over 200 years, is recorded in 1340.

Both the Godsworthy farms together with Broadmoor (now White Tor Stables), Harragrove and Wedlake followed in the next century. Huntingdon, which has now disappeared, lay between Higher Godsworthy and Cox Tor and was occupied by the Holmes family in the middle of the nineteenth century. When the Duke of Bedford rebuilt Harragrove in the 1830s the Holmes family moved there and Huntingdon, which had been the court house for the manor, was allowed to fall into decay.

The famine years of the 1270s and later the Black Death in 1348–50 killed about a third to a half of the population of Devon, including three rectors of Peter Tavy, and led to the abandoning of some of the more remote farms. Wapsworthy, although known by that name as early as 1230, was rebuilt in the 1500s but was originally believed to have replaced a much earlier settlement called Yoledon. The farm at Butterberry in Cudlipptown has never been restored. The recovery of the area was accelerated by the presence of tin ore in the streams above Willsworthy, a factor that must have made these desolate lands more attractive as tin could fetch a high price. A number of farmers responded with farms re-appearing such as that at Standon, where John Chubbe was tinning in 1520, and Brousentor, where the Badcock family lived in 1500.

To this earlier surge of farms, in the seventeenth century, we can assign Youlditch (Ye Olde Ditch) owned by Nicolas Cudlipp and John Edgcumbe but in the tenancy of Peter Cragg, as well as Hilltown, Coppithorne, Tortown and Collaton, though there are indications that some may be older. The farms at Beardown and Bearwalls were enlarged through enclosure by Edward Bray in around 1800. Lanehead, Reddaford and Yellowmead all appear at about this time, although there are good reasons to believe that they too were restorations of earlier settlements.

A great deal of rebuilding took place in the village at the end of the Napoleonic Wars and it is probable that most of the thatched roofs which characterised the villages of Devon were torn down and replaced with slate. The slate quarried in Devon had previously been used but plentiful and cheaper Welsh slate became available. None of the old roofs of either type are now to be seen in the village, perhaps because the opportunity had been taken to add an upper floor to old single-storey cottages whilst re-roofing was taking place. Among the farms central to the village that are recorded at the turn of the eighteenth century are 'old' Churchtown, now Burma House, and Tanglin, and Gatehouse. Much of Wisdom, which may have been a late-medieval farm, was also rebuilt. In 1817 Jonathan Peek who was farming there was taken to the Manor Court for building his house into the public road, a situation that remains to this day! Besides these farms working anything from 30 to 200 acres, many of the cottages were smallholdings of no more than two to ten acres. The occupants of these tenements paid their rent to local landlords and perhaps worked in the mines or quarries during the day, using the weekend and the summer evenings to raise crops, some of which were taken to market in Tavistock or sold within the village. Shula and Southditch were successful examples of this, as was Shillands, the land farmed by the Millers at Higher Mill. For many years the Glebe land could be regarded in this light, but by the time Revd Pocock died in 1722 the 70 acres of land belonging to the church were leased to local farmers.

Agriculture did not fare well in the second half of the nineteenth century. The collapse of the mining industry on which many families had come to depend, led to many farms changing hands. New ideas about farming, changes in methods for breeding stock, emigration of families (or at least the younger members to towns and overseas) led to the development of larger farms. Whereas in 1851 the two Godsworthy hamlets consisted of six farms and a total of 40 inhabitants, by the end of the century this had reduced to three farms with considerably fewer in residence. The process continues with mechanisation enabling fewer men to manage more land and larger numbers of stock. Cox Tor, once a single farm, incorporated Coppithorne, Youlditch and a small tenement called Bew. Chubb Farm was started by Edward Dodd in 1885 and absorbed some of the smallholdings, released by this flight from agriculture to the towns, and land sold by the Duke of Bedford. It has been the only 'new' farm to develop in the last 100 years.

Today as the older farms take on the land released by farmhouses, which are becoming homes for people working in the towns and those looking for peace away from the stress of city life, agriculture goes on steadily supporting village ways and village life. But behind those cottage doors there are increasing numbers of people who have set up a home industry, and who knows what life will come to the village from these changes?

Tin workings above Wedlake (see also page 12).

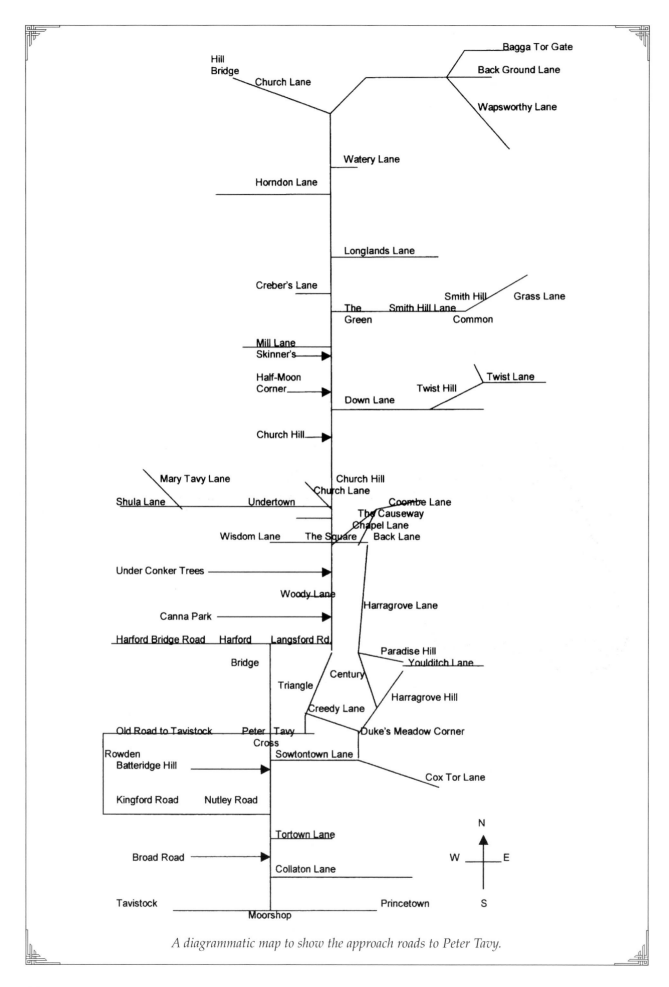

A diagrammatic map to show the approach roads to Peter Tavy.

Roads, Lanes & Bridleways

Patrick Cashell

Approaches to the village, passable by vehicle, may be roughly described as being from the south, south-west and north. Within the village, lanes lead to houses, farms and hamlets and are often named accordingly. Bridleways, paths and tracks link the village with the moor, which is the eastern boundary, and the River Tavy on the western side.

From Moorshop, the crossroads on the Tavistock to Princetown road (B3357), Broad Road brings the visitor from the south. It is conjectured that its name refers to its width in comparison with any other tracks leading to the village. Off this road Collaton Lane to the right leads to farms and houses of that name and extends further, in bridleway form, to the moor below Cox Tor. The next turning to the right is Tortown Lane – a private drive to Tortown. To the left, a little further on, a road leads to the Nutley and Kingford farms, known as Nutley Road coming from the east and Kingford Road from the opposite direction! Ahead is Batteridge Hill which extends as far as Harford Bridge. The origin of the hill's name is unknown but by reason of the numerous accidents which have occurred there, it appears aptly named! Just before the steepest, narrowest and most twisty part of Batteridge Hill, Sowtontown Lane on the right leads as far as Headlands before branching to the right to become Cox Tor Lane. Passing Cox Tor Farm, it becomes a short bridleway before reaching the moor gate below Cox Tor. The left-hand branch leads to another junction with a triangular patch of grass, called Duke's Meadow Corner. Another steep and narrow lane – Creedy Lane (perhaps a vernacular name for it is suggested that it might have been called Creepy Lane, since it saw horses pulling heavy carts, struggling slowly uphill) – drops down towards Batteridge Hill. Northwards from Duke's Meadow Corner, Harragrove Hill leads to Harragrove Farm. To the right, immediately before the farm, Youlditch Lane leads to Youlditch and the moor below Cox Tor. Off Harragrove Hill to the left, a bridleway named Century – or as in the *Glebe Terrier* of the church for 1764, Saintry – crosses fields to link Harragrove Hill and Paradise Hill, named after an adjoining field. From the corner at the bottom of Paradise Hill, Harragrove Lane becomes Back Lane as it enters the village. Back Lane was so-called since it was the back way to Harragrove and was originally no more than a footpath.

The continuation of Batteridge Hill from the Sowtontown Lane turning reaches Peter Tavy Cross, known to many as Radge Cross or 'Crossroads', to the left of which lies the Old Road to Tavistock and opposite, Triangle, a small lane that links Batteridge Hill, the bottom of Creedy Lane and Langsford Road. The Old Road to Tavistock is metalled until a sharp corner above Pitts Cleave Quarry, where it becomes a bridleway called Rowden, leading to a farm of that name and onwards to pass the end of the Nutley–Kingford Road. The signpost at Peter Tavy Cross is interesting in two respects: first, it has the four cardinal points of the compass marked at the top, and second, the inner faces of the arms pointing to the Old Road to Tavistock and the continuation of Batteridge Hill have no directions marked on them. Of course, since these inner faces can only be seen from a field, it must have been thought unnecessary to name them! This crossroads must have been a major junction in early days for old maps indicate two directions at this point – Tavistock and Ashburton.

From the south-west the approach is via Harford Bridge Road, over the bridge itself and, leaving Batteridge Hill on the right, along Langsford Road as far as the farm of that name, where it bends to the left. This road is known as Canna Park, some say Kenny Park, after the name of the field on the right. At the end of a stretch of pavement, Woody Lane, known also as Hoody Lane or Oody Lane, strikes off to the left and leads to fields. The name Woody derives from the trees which once lined the lane and whose branches once covered it – perhaps forming a dark hood. The last stretch into the village is called Under Conker Trees, passing under tall chestnut trees. The traveller arrives in the Village Square and may join Back Lane to the right or, if on foot or horse-back, follow Chapel Lane, which then becomes a bridlepath called either The Causeway or Crossways, which links at the bridge below Higher Mill with Mill Lane. From Higher Mill northwards, Coombe Lane, which becomes a footpath, leads towards the Coombe and the moor. Off the Square to the left is Wisdom Lane, which passes an old farm of that name and what was the Reading Room, before entering meadows. Just before the road crosses the Colley, otherwise known as Peter Tavy Brook by the Village Bridge, a lane to the left, unmarked on definitive maps but classed as a 'county' road, is unnamed and leads to Lower Mill. A little further on, at Gatehouse, the road divides in three ways. To the left, Undertown, deriving its name from the fields, leads to Shula Lane and to the house of that name, off which a bridlepath, Mary Tavy Lane, drops down to the right to Mary Tavy Clam and the River Tavy. Directly ahead, Church Lane leads to St Peter's Church and ahead to the right, Church Hill.

From the north, the traveller has first to come from Mary Tavy, and then pass through Horndon and Willsworthy before crossing the River Tavy at Hill Bridge. The road continues uphill – Hill Bridge Hill or, as Crossing records, Church Lane – to a 'T' junction. The road to the left leads to Wapsworthy. Here a bridleway, Wapsworthy Lane, on the right gives access to Back Ground Lane and the fields at Longbettor as well as the open moor below White Tor. The road continues and to the left Brousentor Lane leads to the farm of that name. The metalled road ends at a moor gate below Bagga Tor, linking there with the Lich Way.

Turning right at the 'T' junction above Hill Bridge, the road leads to Cudlipptown and Peter Tavy. Following this road, off to the left lies a short lane, Watery Lane, along which there is no right of way. At a granite milestone on the right, set in the hedge and inscribed, Tavistock 5 miles, Wapsworthy 1 mile, Horndon ½ mile, a rough bridleway called Horndon Lane leads to Horndon Clam and on over the River Tavy to Horndon. The next lane to the left is Longlands Lane, an accommodation lane to fields below the moor and, again, with no right of way.

At Cudlipptown, a short lane, Creber's, which leads over private property to Coad's Wood and along which there is no right of way, lies to the right of the Green and shortly before a road to the left. This is Smith Hill Lane, which leads across Smith Hill Common to Grass Lane, a bridleway also known as Green Lane and Pack Lane, and to the moor below

White Tor. A common corruption of Smith Hill Lane is Smithy Lane. Before this lane was metalled and re-routed it skirted Smith Hill Tor on its north side, where the ancient track is clearly visible. Further on to the right, Mill Lane, with no right of way, led to the old Devon United Mine, the workings of which lie above the banks of the River Tavy. The narrowest part of the road from Cudlipptown is called Skinner's, after the field it adjoins. Next there is a double bend in the road called Double Bends or Half-Moon Corner. On the approach to Peter Tavy and at the top of Church Hill, to the left is Down Lane, which gives access to Smeardon Down and the moor. Off this metalled lane to the right, a small pathway called South Ditch Lane leads to the cottage of that name and becomes a footpath to the Coombe. To the left just past a quarry, Twist Hill, which after the Second World War became known as Slate or Slatey Hill, having been surfaced by American soldiers with slate and stone from the spoil tips of the Devon United Mine, rises to join Twist Lane on the left. That lane leads to an ancient and now derelict farm of that name. The track now passes through newtakes as Hart Smitten Lane and joins the ancient Peter Tavy Peat Track to reach the open moor.

Older Settlements & Farms in the Parish

Baggator
First records state that this building was occupied in 1219 and this entry is followed by one in the Assize records of 1238, under the name Bacga's tor. From the mid-sixteenth century it was occupied by the Maddaford family and then between 1790–1870 by Andrew Cudlipp and his son Andrew. A William Yeoh followed Captain Palk who, it is claimed, 'being flush with money... bought Baggator Farm' in 1850. Later inhabitants were Reginald Clark after the First World War and William Reed in the 1930s. Alec Phillott recalls that Colonel Worscott was living there at the outbreak of the Second World War. A small galvanised shed where he kept hounds was previously part of a mine complex. When he was called up Miss Pereira who farmed on Vixen Tor took over.

Broadmoor (now White Tor Stables)
The original house was a medieval dwelling in 1400 when Walter Langford was farming there. Walter Cole in 1719, John Holmes in 1815 and Mary Prout in 1863 lived and farmed in the old building. In 1896 Emanuel Watkins was the tenant when, following a fire in 1900, it was completely destroyed. It was rebuilt on a different site and sold to John Rice. Although it was on the market in 1930 John Rice farmed there until 1948 when Harry and Dorothy Homer came. The owners at the time of writing, David and Susan Turner, took over the farm for horse riding from Rod Webb Taylor in 2000.

Beardon and Bearwalls
Situated at the northern extreme of the parish close to the Dartmoor Inn at Lydford, the land of Beardon and Bearwalls was enclosed by Edward Bray in 1790. To serve the two farms he built the bridge over the Cowsic which was washed away in the storms of 1890–91. John Hannaford ran the farms for the Bray family before they were split into Higher and Lower Beardon. Charles Friend took over Higher Beardon, whilst the Bolt and Gill families ran the farm at Lower Beardon and Bearwalls. In 1875 John Cole's family occupied Higher Beardon, but it was put on the market in 1912 with Bearwalls which was being farmed by a Mr Brendon, when Lower Beardon was bought by W.E. Medland.

Brousentor
This old farm, first mentioned in Subsidy returns in 1333 and again in 1403, derives its name from Brown's Don, or Brown's Farm. This was certainly a tinners farm. In 1523 John Badcoke coined a hundredweight of tin at Tavistock. Some 60 years later Walter Brownsdon was presented at Lydford Court for failing to keep the moor gate in good repair. As names go it has had its fair share, being successively Brownson and even Brazen Tor in the first edition of the Ordnance Survey. William Crossing did not help by christening it Brouzen Tor. The Sleeman family lived there between 1851 and 1881, after which it passed into the hands of John and Betsy Wonnacott.

Soon after the war the Harvie family moved there and farmed between 1919 and 1930, until the Fuge family took over. In 2002, the house is occupied by Graham and Katherine Heard, bringing back to Peter Tavy another family name well founded in Devon.

Chubb Farm

The farm, established by Edward Dodd in 1885, was a house originally called The Green, as it stood at one side of the old Village Green. It was the last farm to be established in Peter Tavy. It has remained in the Dodd family and has developed as some smaller farms have ceased to work. The western extension to the house is known as Chubb Lea.

Lower Churchtown

The present Churchtown was built in around 1912 by the Holmes family, in the grounds of the Churchtown Farm. The old farm, now Tanglin and Burma Cottages, was built around 1790 by the Chubb family where one of the sons farmed for many years.

Higher Churchtown

This is one of the early village farms which was in existence in 1280, but little seems to be recorded apart from its involvement in the manor of Huntingdon and ownership by the Dukes of Bedford. Rebuilt in 1818 by the Peek family, it was farmed in recent years by Bill and Mary Bellamy until the 1960s.

Collaton

This farm was also known as Pocock or Peacock and is probably rooted in a medieval farm. However, the renovations done in 1817 were so extensive that almost all evidence was removed or buried under the new work. The farm was clearly of some importance as it was the courthouse for the meetings of Courts Baron and Leet for the manor of Longford. This manor, developed by the Radcliffe family to supervise their lands in Peter Tavy and surrounding parishes, had, prior to 1692, been based in Moore Town where the Langsford family owned it as far back as 1400.

Coppithorne

A small farm of only around 15 acres, the holding probably originates from an enclosure during the sixteenth or seventeenth century. The earliest reference to it is in 1796, when it was owned by the Duke of Bedford and was leased to William Fuge. In 1854 the Duke of Bedford sold the lease to John Cole, whose family farmed there until 1910. Meanwhile, Pollexefen Radcliffe had bought the farm from the Duke. He leased it to George Doidge and when he left the district Francis Bellamy took over the remainder of the lease. In 1948 Francis Bellamy bought the freehold of the farm together with Cox Tor from the Radcliffes.

Brousentor, 1910.

Chubb Farm (previously known as The Green), 1930.

Broadmoor, now White Tor Stables.

Youlditch.

19

Langsford Farm.

Baggator.

Standon.

Higher Wapsworthy.

Coxtor

Probably the oldest surviving building in the parish, Coxtor is still in daily use as a farmhouse. Tests done on ash taken from the centre of the building have recorded dates of around AD850, although the earliest records are only dated to 1216, when the Bowrens paid the lord of the manor a fee to take up residence. By mid 1400 it was part of the manor of Longford under William Langford, and Thomas Ffolynos was farming there in 1572. For some 40 years between 1780 and 1820 Amos and William Reep held tenancy, but in 1835 the Doidge family arrived and remained until 1910 when George Horn took up the farm. In 1932 Francis Bellamy took over the tenancy and subsequently bought the farm from the Radcliffes in 1948.

Coxtor does not seem to have passed with the rest of Longford Manor when it was sold in 1692 to Jasper Radcliffe, for by the early-nineteenth century it was owned by the Parsons family, though the Radcliffes subsequently bought it in 1888.

W.G. Hoskins believes that many farms in Devon were well established by the time of the Norman Conquest but that such farms were subject to attack from neighbours, and in the west of Devon, no doubt, from the Cornish. Farms were therefore built in the manner of Coxtor in a square with a single entrance that would be fortified. Doors to all the barns and even the windows to rooms in the farmhouse open into the central courtyard. Only essential slits to shoot an arrow through faced out on to the moor. This ceased to be important after the twelfth and thirteenth centuries when local warfare was on the wane.

Coxtor also lies close to the moor track from Buckfast Abbey to Tavistock Abbey and a stone cross near the entrance lane suggests that it was a point at which travellers might rest, or monks recovering from an illness might recuperate.

Gate House Farm

Parsons Crossing built this prominent building in the village at the end of the Napoleonic Wars in about 1820. The Roskilly family bought it 20 years later but did not farm from there, letting it out to successive farmers. John Burley's family farmed between 1835–57, followed by John Garland Bray until George Perkins took on the farm in 1874. The Roskillys sold the farm to the Perkins in 1906. George's family continued to farm from Gate House until James Perkins retired in the 1980s and the farm buildings were divided and sold for housing. The farm took its name from an unusual entrance to the yard in the form of a curved granite arch.

Higher and Lower Godsworthy

Both these farms can claim medieval roots with Higher Godsworthy probably claiming Saxon beginnings. The name is derived from the Saxon thegn Gode or Goda, and the suffix, -worthy, indicates a clearance from furze and heather. The earliest reference is in 1244 and may concern tinning rather than farming. By 1408 John Bannock together with John Colmysher and William Gille paid dues to Buckfast Abbey at Godsworthy. They were followed shortly by Robert Reed, specifically at South Godsworthy, which suggests that North or Lower Godsworthy was a separate entity. By 1600 John Ogeblue, John Smerdon and Richard Langfford were tenants under the Duke of Bedford. John Chubb, whose family tenanted and then owned much of the Godsworthy farms over the next 200 years, joined them in 1608. Some of the land seems to have changed hands frequently and by the end of the seventeenth century some 13 separate tenants were rated by the Parish Council. Some idea of the complications in land dealings can be gathered from the need to refer in one document to 'holding seven parts of a forty-eighth division' of the land in question! However, all was not lost and at Higher Godsworthy Henry Reddicliffe bought the portions owned by Roger Chubb's family and those of the Revd Edward Spencer, who died in 1907. The latter had been responsible for unwinding all the smallholdings and drawing them into a single farm of some 35 acres.

Meanwhile, the Chubb family were also tenants at Lower or North Godsworthy in 1608. At the end of the eighteenth century the farm was partly owned by Ann and Edgcumbe Parsons. George Chubb and John Vogwill (snr and junr) were now in occupation. In 1867 the Parsons family sold the farm to William Stevens, a cattle dealer, who in turn sold it to George Henry Abel in 1888. George Abel's family have farmed both farms since shortly after the Second World War, when Cyril Abel bought the land which was previously in the hands of the Reddicliffes at Higher Godsworthy.

Harragrove

This was a medieval farm, recorded in 1412 when it was farmed by John Maynarde for the Abbey at Tavistock. It passed into the hands of the Dukes of Bedford after the Reformation and was the courthouse for the manor of Huntingdon when farmed by the Prout and Holmes families in the eighteenth century. It was purchased by the Bellamy family during the twentieth century.

Hilltown

Hilltown, or Hillsdown, was built in the early part of the seventeenth century when George Beare of St Truan in Cornwall owned it. It was leased to the Condy family but came into the hands of the Moores of Moortown, who later sold it to Jasper Radcliffe, when he bought the property in the manor of Longford in 1692. After a period in the hands of the Tremaynes, it was sold to the Roskilly family at the beginning of the nineteenth century, but they did not keep it for long, selling to the Reeps by 1824. The Rice family had land there from an early date and decided to come to live there around 1700. One of the Harvie

family came to farm and provide accommodation for visitors towards the end of the nineteenth century.

Langsford

A corruption of the word 'langskaryford', which in early English referred to a point distant from the Parish Church, this farm is old and was occupied by Walter Langsford in 1325. A John Jele of Langsford appears among those listed as tinners at Willsworthy in 1523. It came into the Parsons family by 1672 and 100 years later Sarah Parsons leased the farm to Peter Reddicliffe. During the ownership of the Parsons family the farm appears on maps as 'The Parsonage'. It is not clear at what point it reverted to its former name. Much of the house was rebuilt in 1822. By 1841 James Crossing had come to live there and his son James Parsons Crossing followed him. Thomas Roskilly bought the farm in 1877 and several members of his family lived and farmed from there before Randolph Simmons took over in 1948.

Longbettor

Longbettor, or Longbetter, was a small farm of unknown age above Wapsworthy, but was probably enclosed after earlier tinning had died down. William Ballard recalls how his family came to farm there in 1924. The owners, the Dawe family of Bere Ferrers, kept a large flock of sheep on the common land, but the Ballards had no more than a few sheep and beef cattle with a cow to provide their domestic milk. The weekly income came from the butter, cream, eggs and oven-ready poultry his mother took to market in Tavistock each Friday. In the summer the Dawe family would come up to the farm with lots of strawberries and at Christmas with a large tin of chocolates. Peggy Stephens recalls her childhood there and how they were the last family to live at the house.

Radge

Radge is a very old farm, technically not in the parish of Peter Tavy but in Tavistock. Most of those farming at Radge have been associated with the village rather than the town. Records suggest that even in 1380, when a Walter Raddish farmed there, it was regarded as well established. It was well known for being the property of Revd Thomas Larkham who bought it in 1658 to support his reactionary views on the Church and Parliament. While he was the vicar of Tavistock he was banned by his colleagues in surrounding parishes from preaching in their churches, and so held meetings in the private homes of those who supported him. He had returned from America with Dissenting views of the established Church and wished to reform it.

The Mary Dean Charity that supported the school of that name at Tamerton Ffoliot purchased Radge Farm in 1734. They retained the ownership until Mrs May Wakeham (née Medland), who was born at the farm, bought it from them.

Sowtontown

Known originally as South Town due to its position south of the village, it is mentioned in Assize papers as early as 1249. Ralph de Southetown lived there in 1332, but it had passed to the Kinge family before the Radcliffes bought it in 1720. It was later sold to the Parsons before the Cole family and the Mudge family came to live there in the seventeenth century.

Stannon

Stannon, or more properly Standon, lies well into the moor and has a history extending back to around 1000BC. A village of some 40 huts has been identified through pottery fragments and cooking stones. It may well have been deserted during the cold period before early medieval times. Tinners and farmers returned early in the twelfth century and by 1572 William Standon had paid a £10 fine for a lease, '... for by Godd's sufferance, I interditte to marry and take to wyffe Elinor Rychards.' In 1597 Ellynor Standon, a widow, was passing the land on to her children Joan, wife of Robert Kynge of Peter Tavy, and Henry Standon. In the eighteenth century a Mr Collier built an extension to the house. Stannon is within the military range and in 1977 most of the building was burnt down.

Wapsworthy

Also known as Warpesworthie, or even Waspsworthy, this is one of the oldest hamlets in the parish. There were three farms, though one has now almost completely disappeared, and the other two are not farmhouses. It has been suggested that the present site was built on when the settlers returned after the severe climatic conditions eased around 1100. A previous name for the site was Youlden, Ye Old Don or Farm. John Fitzrichard was living there in 1280 and it has been continuously occupied since. In 1939 William (Bill) Harvie lived there with his wife Emma. Bill had a tendency to drop off to sleep and Emma was always having to 'rose' him. In those days 'dunging' the fields was done by hand, dropping a spade full every so many paces. Emma would call out, 'nother here Bill', then pace forward and call again. If she thought he had not heard or was not paying attention she would call out 'Ain't that right Bill?'

Wedlake

First mentioned in the Court Rolls of 1400 when Walter Wydelake held the land, Henry Wyllington was living there in 1557. 'Lake' is an Old English name for a stream or small river, but does the 'Wed' derive from the corruption of 'white', or 'wide'? By 1692 it was part of the Longford Manor estates that were bought by the Radcliffe family, who sold the farm and land to George Paige. It was subsequently farmed by the Mudge family of Collaton with William Bellamy acting as hind. William Bellamy bought the farm in 1919 and it has remained in that family since.

Wisdom

This has always been a small farm in the middle of the village. Apparently of early origins, parts of the buildings were thought to be of medieval structure but now no longer exist. It was rebuilt in 1815 by the Prout family who were taken to the Manor Court for allowing the wall of the house to protrude into the highway. It still does! Wisdom has been the centre of many activities whilst in the hands of the Bray family, from farm, to Post Office, to shop. Mrs Ida Lynd (née Bray) was the last of that family to live there, seeing in her long life the disappearance of the small farm and the changes towards tourism. She died in 1996 at the age of 95 years.

Youlditch

Similarly derived from 'Ye Old Ditch', the house was probably not built until the seventeenth century and was tenanted by the Crag family until 1721, when the owner Nicolas Cudlipp came to live there. The Vear family, also from Cudlipptown, lived there for a short period before the Phillips family came in 1824. They were to remain farming there until 1970.

Radge.

Higher Godsworthy, 1920s. Outside the porch of the old long house. Left to right: *Harry Williams, John Reddicliffe, Mary Williams, Walter Reddicliffe.*

TWO COATS COLDER THAN TAVISTOCK

The Colley Brook rises above Wedlake and gathers pace as it comes down through the Coombe to reach the village. Early restrictions with small waterfalls and languid pools do nothing to halt it. By the time it reaches the bridge in the centre of the village, any rise in the water level fills the archway.

The south coast of Devon is known for sunshine and seaside holidays, but Dartmoor is higher and as the air rises so the temperature drops and the rain descends. So Dartmoor is known for the bogs and the mists, which despite the wind can persist for quite long periods. The site for the village of Peter Tavy was well chosen by our forefathers who recognised the benefits of the protection afforded by Smear Ridge to the north and the line of tors from Cox Tor to Great Mis Tor to the south and east. Despite such natural protection, when the temperature drops in the winter and the snow comes down the valley, substantial drifts are formed. In March 1891 the snow was accompanied by strong winds with drifts up to 10 or 12 feet. In more recent years we have been luckier, but some of the accompanying pictures show the lane out of Peter Tavy to Cudlipptown after the blizzards of 1984. Several villagers remember walking to work on the top of the hedges and many farms on the moor were cut off for one or two weeks. In the winter of 1947–48 the snow was so heavy that the village was completely cut off. For six to eight weeks, and even longer, some farms on the moor were without contact. James Perkins recalled an earlier blizzard in 1927, when drifting snow blocked his access to stock in the shippen at Gatehouse Farm and he had to dig his way in. There is always an up side to such weather and children unable to get to school found other things to fill the time. Snowmen have been a regular sight in the Square and toboggans are usually quick to appear.

It is not only snow which causes problems, for placed as it is at the junction of the Colley Brook with

Above: *The floods of 1890 washed away an archway of Harford Bridge.*

Left: *At Mary Tavy Clam this more substantial bridge was built to replace the Clam that was a victim of the floods in 1880 and was washed away in 1890.*

This view from the top of the Village Bridge shows how the force of water moves stones and branches, which are occasionally responsible for blocking the flow and flooding the village.

The view from Harford Bridge in 1991, looking up the Tavy, showing the extensive flooding of the fields, which drain quickly as the water level on the river falls.

The temporary wooden bridge, which was used while the archway on Harford Bridge was rebuilt. It was still there in 1892.

Snow on the banks of the Colley Brook, 1984.

Above: *Snowmen in the Square. Their appearance is a regular occurrence as soon as snow falls.*

Left: *The road to Cudlipptown, winter 1983/4.*

View from the garden of Lower Mill, 1964.

the Tavy, the village's experience of floods has been a regular occurrence, especially if rain follows the melting of snow. The Tavy holds the reputation for being the fastest-flowing river on Dartmoor and rises very quickly, only to fall almost as fast. In the floods of 1880 Hillbridge and Mary Tavy Clam were both washed away.

On the night of 16 July 1890 over two inches of rain fell in a matter of a few hours. Much of west Dartmoor was flooded, but the Tavy and its tributaries took the brunt, with levels rising by up to eight to ten feet.

Peter Tavy duly received its share. Mrs Prout, living in what was then Churchtown Farm, now Tanglin and Burma House, could not get down her staircase for the water and the six children of the Darke family had to be rescued from an upstairs window. Mrs Stacey in Rose Cottage was also flooded. A complete archway of Harford Bridge was washed away and a temporary wooden bridge was the only available crossing for many months to come. The old road passing Radge Farm was still in regular use at this time by people going to Tavistock so this was not the inconvenience it seemed at first. John Cole, farming at Harford Farm, found that part of his house had disappeared and the railway beyond was completely submerged, as was a great part of the new road to Tavistock. The Clam at Mary Tavy was again washed away, effectively isolating the village from the west side of the Tavy, and both the clapper bridge and the road bridge at Beardown suffered.

There was no bridge opposite Higher Mill, only a ford, but the Clam in the Coombe was washed down.

In spite of its importance for access to Merrivale, where the road bridge had also been washed away, it does not seem to have been repaired for some weeks. It may be that the Colley Brook changed its course at this time, or perhaps the change was due to cost, for these were bad times for the farmers and the mines of the area were steadily closing down. As for the bridge at Higher Mill, that was not erected until 1894–5 after William Williams, the miller, had been asked by the Parish Council 'to seek funds from well-disposed people to pay for it'.

On the moor there are more problems, even when the winter has passed and the spring rains have stopped, as Cyril Abel relates. Early in the summer of 1989 he and his sons went out to the pass at Sandy Hole where a cow had fallen through a crust of earth that had dried in the sun and was struggling in a deep pool of water underneath.

Snow at Cudlipptown Green. The heaviest snow in recent years cut off most of the farms on the moor past Cudlipptown.

Removing ice from the River Tavy at Hillbridge, 1932.

Above: *Cutting corn at Nutley, early 1920s. John Maynard Roskilly is on the binder. Left to right: Charles, Kitty (née Roskilly), Barbara and Jack Bunsell, Kathleen (later Simmons) and Joyce Roskilly.*

Right: *Bred by Cyril and Eileen Abel, Glenuig was a champion Scotch blackface ram for a number of years at the Devon County Show in the 1960s. Shown here with Eileen in 1968.*

Shearing at Higher Godsworthy, 1929. Left to right, back row: Harry Palmer, Harold Cunningham, Henry Northmore, Horace Geak, Harry Williams, Loftus Dodd, John Reddicliffe, Walter Reddicliffe, George Abel; front row: Reg Reddicliffe, Harold Vogwill, Arthur Mudge, Jack Reddicliffe, Jack Mudge, Edward Dodd.

Frederick William Dodd sawing up logs with a circular saw borrowed from Bawden's of Horrabridge.

Edward Dodd makes short work of shearing a sheep, 1996.

Weighing the wool before baling, 1930s.

This rather rusty and frail looking peat cutter on a 5ft handle has done sterling work in its time. Note the blade at right angles on just one side; this prevented the wet peat sticking in the cutter.

Cutting peat in the 1930s. A long tie was worked from above and below, and the faggots stacked to dry over summer. They were brought down in the autumn after harvest and were stacked under cover if possible. A slightly damp faggot would last longer, so care was taken to ensure they were not over-dried.

Below: John Bellamy drives a flock of sheep through the village in 1983. This occurrence is seen less often today as flocks are moved more readily by lorry.

Farming

Peter Tavy owes much to farmers and farming. Areas to the east of Roos Tor suggest that the earliest settlers cleared the ground for cultivation as long ago as 2000BC and, as the poor ground deteriorated from lack of fertilisation, they moved on to clear other sites. A Bronze-Age settlement on the west side of Whit Tor shows a number of hut circles enclosed by a perimeter wall. Perhaps the wall kept cattle or sheep from straying at night or, more likely, kept them out to protect the garden plots where small amounts of vegetables were being cultivated. Even larger settlements on Standon Hill and Roos Tor show similar irregular low walls between houses. These are the early signs of the hunter-gatherer settling to become the farmer of today. Evidence from studies done at Coxtor Farm indicate that people were living there in the ninth century AD. By the time of the Domesday Survey in 1086 a Saxon called Siward was farming at Willsworthy and at Peter Tavy itself. He possessed land for 7 ploughs, with pasture 16 furlongs long by 9 furlongs wide, and there was a population of about 20.

Building a hayrick, c.1910.

The suffix '-worthy' in so many place names implies land that has been cleared and the era in which this occurred on Dartmoor was during the eleventh and twelfth centuries. By the end of the twelfth and into the thirteenth century the farming settlements of Godsworthy, Willsworthy and Cudlipptown with several others found in the Domesday Book, were well established. Past leaders of the settlements giving their names to places, like Gode to Godsworthy and Cudda's lype or crossing to Cudlipptown, suggest even earlier communities. Whilst these twelfth-century settlers were primarily sheep and cattle farmers, they also had an interest in the tin to be found in the gravel of the rivers and streams that are around here. Peter Tavy cannot claim to have been at the forefront of the tin industry, although considerable quantities were obtained between the twelfth and fifteenth centuries, particularly above Willsworthy. Much of the moor around Peter Tavy remains pock-marked by the work of these prospective miners.

Away from the central forest of Dartmoor the settlements first organised into manors and parishes by the Saxons have retained their right to cut peat, turf and fern, to pasture cattle upon the common land and to quarry stone. Farm economy over the centuries has been closely dependent upon these rights, for the moors are a wilderness – rocky, wet and much of it above 1,000ft – not the best conditions to grow food, but at its best able to sustain the hardier of animals.

Sheep probably came with the earliest settlers and among artefacts that have been found in Cudlipptown is a Bronze-Age stone spindle whorl for spinning wool. Cattle and ponies must have been introduced at a very early stage to supply the power to draw ploughs for cultivation of the land and to supply meat, milk and dairy produce. Ponies were an inescapable necessity for carrying loads over land, where the wheel was a latecomer. The story is still told of William Reep of Coxtor and later of Hill Town, reputed to have been the first in Peter Tavy to take a wheeled cart on to the moor. He suffered so much ridicule from his neighbours and so many problems with the cart that he unharnessed his horse and left the vehicle to rot on Langstone Moor. William Reep died in the 1860s, but it was still some years before the wheel was a common sight. Reep, like his colleagues, was on the moor to cut peat which was an essential fuel for the massive hearths, and one for which a good trade could be found in the towns.

Fern was used extensively for animal bedding and was cut from the moor in large quantities. Some farmers still use it as a cheap alternative to straw, but only where it can be easily harvested by tractors and mowing machines. There are problems, as 'Bill' Bellamy of Coxtor explained. He lost one of his best calves from a perforation of the gullet when bedded on fern and it can be poisonous if eaten in quantity.

Pasture is the greatest boon to the moor farmer as it enables him to turn his sheep and cattle out to graze while the fields are used to grow hay or silage for the winter. Sheep were kept in large numbers and farmers went out on the moor at the end of each week to clear their leer (or lear) of 'foreign' sheep. (Leer is a locally-used word to mean the area on the moor to which the majority of any flock of sheep or herd of cattle will go naturally when turned loose. It is apparently an inherited characteristic and was one of the disasters of 'Foot and Mouth' when

Four of thirteen stone niches for the skip beehives that were used at Radge Farm to raise bees for honey. Now overgrown with rock plants, they make a pretty hedge.

Scots Galloway cattle on the moor.

whole flocks were slaughtered and there were no ewes to pass this on. Lear is possibly a corruption of the word 'layer'. Interestingly, even a short distance away northwards the word used is 'hefted'. The authors have no idea where that comes from, but it means lear!) Persistently offending farmers who allowed their sheep or cattle to stray were presented to the Manor Courts as late as the 1920s. The Old Devonshire dim-faced, flat-sided, coarse-boned sheep, with its crooked back and coarse wool, was the standard animal kept until early in the nineteenth century. However, today most of the sheep are either Scotch Blackfaced, Whitefaced Dartmoor or Cheviot. George Abel brought his first Blackfaced sheep to Lower Godsworthy in 1918, but it was not until the 1960s that his grandson Cyril and wife Eileen won the first of their prizes for a champion ram at the Devon County Show. Farmers take a close interest in keeping the hardy crosses and those that put weight on early, but the fleece is now of such low value that moor farmers scarcely

James Perkins of Gatehouse Farm, 1959.

consider it. Yet Dick Friend and Molly Cummings both recall how, as children, they combed the fields for wool before the shearing, and then sold it for a shilling a pound pocket money or spun it into thread for knitting. The hand shearing of sheep by teams of local farmers was a major social occasion on the farm, with local gossip doing the rounds as they moved from farm to farm. The introduction of an engine in the early 1950s, often a 1hp Lister with two shearing heads, was frowned upon as the men could no longer hear each other speak over the noise of the motor.

Shearing was usually completed in May when the competitions would start, each farm taking its turn to host the local final, the winner moving on to the group final until the county final was held at the County Show. James Perkins of Gatehouse Farm was particularly skilled at shearing and made a special point of showing his Exmoor horned sheep as he had the only flock in the village.

Cattle probably came to the moor with the early settlers along with sheep and goats, the black cattle referred to in old writings probably deriving from the native Welsh Mountain cattle. The present black Highland cattle were introduced to the moor about 1900, but George Abel of Godsworthy brought his first Galloways to Peter Tavy in 1930. They stand out against the grass unlike the South Devons, with their warm chestnut colour, that are more widely kept. This animal has been on Dartmoor for many generations and seems to have been bred from a North

Devon crossed with an Old Marlborough red, and is said to have originated in South Molton. It is seen on most Peter Tavy farms today as it is a dependable dual-purpose beast, farmed for both beef and milk.

Until the 1980s several farmers supplied milk directly to the villagers, Frank Collins, Bill Dodd, James Perkins, Frank Northey and Tommy Lynd amongst them. Others tell of having the milk ready by 7a.m., after the morning milking, for the pick-up lorry to collect the churns from the stand at the farm gate. Direct sales became uneconomical with the national adoption of dairy refrigeration, bulk pasteurisation and stricter hygiene regulations; today milk from wholesale distributors is the only milk available. Jessie Bellamy speaks of the cream, butter and eggs that she took to market in Tavistock and sold to friends whom she had arranged to meet there.

Edward and Harriet Dodd, grandparents of Bill Dodd at Chubb Farm, like most farmers, kept enough pigs to kill one or two each week for Plymouth market. It was not just farmers who kept pigs, for many smallholders with little more than an acre would keep at least one pig which they would kill for home consumption when fattened. Pigs are not reliable animals and Cyril Abel of Godsworthy recalls how his father kept pigs at Twist in the 1930s but gave them up, apart from a few for home fare, after one got amongst some lambs and killed them.

There is little arable farming within the parish. The moor is unsuitable for cereal and most fields are needed to grow hay or silage for the winter. A team of men working with scythes, standing diagonally behind each other, mowed the hay. The youngest was at the front of the team and the eldest at the back. This scheme was sometimes used when mowers were first introduced with the men drawing on a long rope attached to the mower or plough. However, when one farmer tried to introduce a mechanical mower in the 1920s some of the labourers went to the field the night before and planted iron pegs in the ground. These broke the blades and made the mowers useless. Collection of the hay by hand gave way to bailers at much the same time; horses drew them and even the smallest of smallholdings had a pony for the trap and a horse to work.

Bill Bellamy recalled that the first tractor on Coxtor Farm arrived in 1943. It was a Fordson with steel rims and they bought rubber tyres for it in 1948, changing to a Ferguson with a mower in 1953.

During the Second World War many farmers were required to plough up part of their land for potatoes or corn and Frank Collins recounted how he grew corn in Coombefields, which was cut and threshed on a machine powered by a belt from the back wheel of George Abel's lorry. Phyllis Dodd remembers the potatoes in Chubb Meadow, stored and over-wintered under corrugated-iron sheets against the hedge. A few acres are still planted with root crops of swede, mangols and green crops of kale or flatpoles that provide winter feed for animals.

Land was not always confined to root crops and greens. The trade directories of 1893 state that the 'chief crops of the parish are oats and barley', though by 1914 this had changed and the same directories report that the 'land is in pasture'. Border farms, such as Radge and Nutley, grew corn much later than this but further on to the moor little corn could be grown because of the cold and wet. Nevertheless, the village supported two grist mills, neither of which ceased working until the early years of the twentieth century. The great agricultural depression of the 1880–90s, when farmers in Peter Tavy would return from market without selling a single animal, followed the fall in the price of corn resulting from cheaper imports. This had led to a switch to cattle and pasture around the margins of the moor, which in turn led to a glut on the market that was also importing meat from the Empire. The high price of corn at the end of the seventeenth century provided the money to build the north aisle of the church,

whereas the earlier rebuilding in the fourteenth and fifteenth centuries had depended on the price of wool used for the cloth-making industry, then booming in Devon. It is a healthy farming environment that the village has depended upon to protect it against the worst of worldwide recessions over the centuries, whether this income be from tin, copper or farming itself.

Demand for food grew with the Industrial Revolution. The population of Plymouth increased by 30,000 in the first half of the nineteenth century. Tavistock, reflecting the growth in mining, increased in population threefold, only to decline again by the end of the century. Peter Tavy was different; many of those recorded in the 1851 Census as miners were in fact smallholders with a part-time interest in mining, which supplemented the household income and to some extent provided for their families. Others were sons and daughters of large families, who, as mining declined, left the parish, to go overseas to America, Australia and South Africa or to the coal mines of South Wales or the north country. As one Peter Tavy emigrant replied when asked why he had left such a beautiful area, 'beauty don't feed no children'.

Nor was farming the reserve of the men. Martha Lethbridge recalls how as children they were given fire shovels to go into the fields before the grass was cut and level the mole hills to prevent them choking

James Perkins on horseback, with John Garland Perkins his father at the Gatehouse.

the finger-beam grass machine that was drawn by two horses. During the First World War two of the bedrooms at Sowtontown were taken over to store and keep the corn dry. Butter was made by hand and it was up to the children to help their mother; in hot weather they took the cream down to the stream to be kept cool.

Apart from rearing sheep, cattle and pigs, Peter Tavy was also renowned for its honey. Today only a few farms and a very few householders keep bees, but in the mid 1900s many homes possessed hives. They sold the honey at the market in Tavistock and around the village and presumably it was worthwhile, but even they were not in the same class as the farmers' wives at Radge. Here it was done on a larger scale with straw skips sitting in a row along the garden walls. It is now many years since the walls saw any hives but the niches remain to provide the stories.

Peat was a basic requirement of everyone living on and around Dartmoor. The right to dig peat from the moor was one of the earliest demands of farmers, tinners and villagers. Its importance to Peter Tavy may be judged by the Peter Tavy Peat Track that runs from just north of the village, over Smeardon Down to rise up to the foot of Whit Tor and onward to the peat beds east of Great Mis Tor. For generations people from all around have cut their peat here, some for domestic use but many taking it to sell in local towns. Some families and some villages had their own 'ties' on which they alone could cut peat. It was cheap so long as your time and your labour were not counted as they are these days. In 1800 100 faggots of peat sold for 13 shillings in the towns, so there were pennies to be made. It was not a quick result, for the peat had to partially dry out before it could be used and was therefore stacked on the moor to drain during the summer and brought down in the autumn to be finished under cover. In 1984 Charles Mudge showed a new generation just what hard work it was when he took a party to the 'Reddicliffe ties' on Langstone moor. Even before cutting the peat itself a top layer of immature peat and grass had to be cut away. This was not wasted; known as 'vags' or half a 'vaggot', these cuts were kept for home use.

Perhaps surprisingly the number of farms in the parish changed little for another 100 years. Today it would be easy to believe that all the farms were always on the moor, but in 1851 of the 29 farms in the parish only five were farming over 100 acres and seven were within the village. As late as 1939 this number had scarcely changed, but as the new millennium started there were only a dozen farms in the whole parish, with just one remaining within the village. The sad thing is that the loss of these farms has meant the loss of the families that ran them, and that is what has changed the face of rural life.

Mining & Quarrying

Besides its agricultural uses the land around Peter Tavy has been extensively exploited for peat, granite and the numerous metal ores contained therein. Tin and copper are the constituents of bronze but there is little evidence that they were mined on Dartmoor in prehistoric times. By the twelfth century, however, the extraction of tin in the brooks and rivers above Peter Tavy was underway and it is now impossible to walk anywhere on the moor without seeing evidence of this activity, which rose to a crescendo in the seventeenth century and slowly faded thereafter.

Stannary records show that the miners streaming tin above Willsworthy in the sixteenth century brought their tin to Tavistock for 'coinage' and taxation in significant amounts. In June 1523 four miners from Peter Tavy – Richard Standon, Richard Elforth, John Cole and John Holwyll, with John Badcoke, John Knight, and John Chubbe from Willsworthy – registered 23 hundredweight between them. The land around the newtakes at Wedlake shows the continuing interest of farmer-miners into the middle of the eighteenth century, though by this time probably more in expectation than success.

In recent years examination of the Walkham above Merrivale, on the parish boundary, shows extensive tin workings that also gave employment to villagers, as did the Merrivale granite quarry. Before the First World War, Frankie Warren lived at Mill Cottages in Peter Tavy and used to go by horse and trap to Merrivale, or walk up over Peter Tavy Coombe, Sharpitor, Godsworthy Plain, between Roos and Staple Tors and down to the quarry. White quartz stones placed on the track over Staple Tor helped the quarrymen to reach their work on dark nights and misty mornings. The Census of 1851 shows an upsurge in miners that had been attracted to the village; not for tin at this time, but copper and in later years for arsenic. Many of these men worked well outside the parish and were known to walk far into the moor where they might stay for most of the week before returning to their families at the weekend.

Situated as a gateway to the moor, the village could hardly have escaped involvement in the deeper mines of the eighteenth and nineteenth centuries. Perhaps surprisingly, apart from the three Devon United mines on the east bank of the Tavy which were begun around 1840 and closed down in 1922, and the mines at Hillbridge and Harford Bridge, Peter Tavy seems to have been mostly affected by the

456

All Sales subject to War. Strikes and other Stoppages.

Dartmoor Granite
for
Monumental Work.
Kerb and Channel.

※

Concrete Blocks,
Kerbs, Paving Slabs,
Fence Posts.

Blue Elvan Roadstone & Chippings in all sizes

To HOARE BROTHERS,

A. S. HOARE.   H. T. LANGSFORD.

Head Office—
PITTS CLEAVE QUARRY,
TAVISTOCK.

Telegrams : Dolerite.
'Phone : Tavistock.
Telephones :
    Tavistock   54.
    Plympton   203.

Tarmacadam Works,
Marsh Mills,
Plympton.

G. Abel. Esqr.
Godsworthy, Peter Tavy   Date   *10th April 1933.*

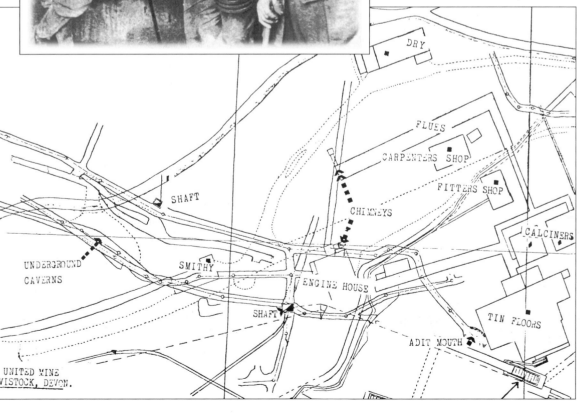

Above: *A billhead from Hoare Brothers at Pitts Cleave, 1933.*

Left: *Three quarrymen at Pitts Cleave. Bert Moyse (centre) died in an accident at the quarry.*

Below: *Plan of Devon United south mine, c.1900.*

drawing of water from the Tavy and other rivers and streams to provide the water power and processes of extraction for the ores. Reddaford Leat took water at the top of Tavy Cleave to Wheal Jewell reservoir for the mines in Mary Tavy. Another leat at Hillbridge takes water to the reservoir for the power station at Mary Tavy to this day.

One more mine of which little is known is Wheal Union, centred on the fields between Pitts Cleave and Harford Bridge. Again it seems to have gone out of production by the middle of the nineteenth century.

As mining declined, men from Peter Tavy left the village to employ their skills overseas. Some of those who went to seek their fortunes were Arthur Sleeman and Bert Rickard who went to Brazil, and Tom Vogwill, who worked in the mines of South Africa and South America. Some found they did not enjoy being so far from home. A tale was told by James Perkins that Harold Vogwill 'took a pasty out with him and brought a corner back'. He didn't stay long!

Devon United Mines

Crossing recounts that the Devon United north mine, previously called East Wheal Friendship, was worked for copper and had been inactive since 1850, but that the central and south mines, previously known as Wheal Ann, were sunk in 1900. The shafts there go down some 27 fathoms (162 feet) and the captain in the earliest days claimed that he could raise ten tons of tin ore a month. The Devon United south mine had extensive workings that reached from the riverside to the land under the Cudlipptown road and under the fields on the east. Here the working conditions were regarded as good under the management of Mr Bowhay who lived in Ivy Cottage. The men going underground were paid by the day and worked eight-hour shifts, around the clock, starting at six in the morning. The men above the surface, working on crushing and smelting, were treated differently.

All the ore from both mines was brought to the south mine on tramways and processed for tin, copper and arsenic on the site. Crossing tells us that about 35 men were employed who were living locally. Amongst these men was Arthur Bellamy's grandfather, who on return from America worked at

A derelict waterwheel used at Devon United mine to generate power – both electricity and compressed air.

The buildings of Devon United mine, 1914. Although none of these are now visible, some of the capped shafts and an engine house can be found.

Below: *One of the old leats on Smeardon that served the Ochre mine, spring 1996. Snow can still be seen on the moor in the distance.*

Above: *Settling tanks, which existed here at the side of the old lane on Smeardon, form part of the Ochre mine. Such tanks needed a great deal of water and leats were built to bring water from the Colley, as well as the springs on the Down. When it was released it was taken alongside the hedge in the field opposite to link up with Higher Mill Leat and back into the Colley Brook. It is not surprising that Miller Williams complained about the water staining his mill-wheel.*

The English China Clay Company, comprising many of the quarries previously owned by Hoare & Brothers, took over Pitts Cleave. Albert Hoare and Bert Langsford (centre right) are shaking hands with the Managing Director of ECC. The majority of the people present are from ECC. Note the large storage sheds for the bins in the background, and on the left the Nissen huts put up by the REMEs during the Second World War.

Devon United drilling the holes in the rocks for explosive charges at a halfpenny a hole. He worked with a steel crowbar specially adapted with a swelling halfway along the shaft with which to get a firmer grip. William John Phillott, like many others, worked at Merrivale part time, as well as running his smallholding of 30 acres at Higher Creason. An interesting discovery was the evidence of gun-metal pipes that conveyed centrally compressed air for their pneumatic drills from Mary Tavy Clam almost to Cudlipptown.

At the west end of Smear Ridge above the village another quite separate mine has left its scars. Helen Harris writes that between about 1840 and 1860 there is documentary evidence of an intention to set up a mine for ochre, but subsequently the printed word is silent. Yet the evidence of a working mine is there, complete with several leats and settling tanks. The late Frank Collins, whose family has lived at Higher Mill for 160 years, recalled hearing his relatives speak of 'ochre pits'. The water-wheel at the mill was stained yellow when they released the water from the settling tanks into the mill leat lying directly below. An extensive water system is still visible on the south and west sides of the Down for water taken from the Colley Brook and the numerous springs amongst the rocks on the Down.

Pitts Cleave

Pitts Cleave opened as a quarry after the First World War, when it had been used as a firing range. James Perkins remembers that there was blasting at the quarry every day at 1p.m. – and that the noise would rattle the windows of the farmhouse at Gatehouse. Albert Hoare and his brother set up the Tavistock Concrete Block company at Pitts Cleave in the early 1930s, making all sorts of pre-cast concrete products, from garden seats to window lintels and fence posts, from the small stone left from dressing the bigger pieces being quarried. Bert Langsford, another partner, seems to have joined a little later and between them they developed a number of quarries around Dartmoor, supplying the stone for Fernworthy Reservoir and other major projects. The stone was a local Blue Elven, a hard basalt rock used widely to make roadstone and tarmacadam.

In the Second World War a camp of Nissen huts was built in the grounds at Pitts Cleave and a company of Royal Electrical and Mechanical Engineers was stationed there. The Army would sometimes put up cricket or football teams to play against the local villages – Peter Tavy was particularly renowned for beating the Army team at Tug o' War and, in 1944, at football. The Nissen huts were used for storage after the Army left but like the canteen buildings they

A group of unidentified quarrymen at Pitts Cleave in 1938.

lay alongside the river and were subject to flooding. Tales are still told of how the workmen's enamel mugs, hanging in the canteen, bore the teeth marks of the river rats.

At its height in the early 1950s more than 100 men were employed at Pitts Cleave, most of them coming from Tavistock and Mary Tavy. Gerald White, Clem Saye, Ken Sillick, Gordon Stephens and Mike Guest are well remembered, particularly as some of them would sing as they walked down the road and over Harford Bridge. So too are the Rice brothers, Cecil, Bill and Harold. Cecil, nicknamed 'Bungay' Rice, in particular was a large man with strong muscles and Ron Cubitt recalls how he always came out top on piecework schedules. He had to cut the stone from the face, break it up into manageable sizes with a 14lb sledgehammer and then load it onto a wagon, which he would push by hand from the quarry face to the weighbridge near the gate, about 200 yards, to have the weight recorded against his name. It is said that when some Polish men stayed on after the war they held competitions but 'Bungay' always won. Earlier workers at the quarry were Bert Moyse from Lower Mill, who sadly lost his life in an accident there, and Bert Maunder who lived at Shula. Mike Guest, remembered here in the village for his photography and chairmanship of the Parish Council, is recalled at Pitts Cleave for his outspoken support of the workmen in the quarry.

Early in 1960 a disagreement broke out because the quarry was undermining the old Tavistock road, running past Radge to Mount Tavy. After a full public inquiry, the first 'loop' was constructed, moving the road south, but this was insufficient and a second 'loop' road had to be made. Some claimed that the road was never used and others argued that it should be preserved as it was the original medieval road, running from Tavistock Abbey to Peter Tavy, before the mines were discovered and the road from Mary Tavy was built. The line of the old road can still be distinguished as it makes its way through an avenue of trees to the quarry edge.

The 1970s saw the start of the running down of the quarry. The firm had now merged with several others in Devon and Cornwall and was to give rise to the English China Clay Company. Other quarries were producing at lower cost and by 1976 many of the workmen had moved to other quarries or found alternative jobs. A few remained on maintenance and a depot was kept there for several years. Stone was brought for dressing from other quarries but seldom in sufficient quantities to justify keeping the quarry open. Final closure, however, did not come until 1992.

Some Peter Tavy Families

Abel

George Henry Abel came to Lower Godsworthy from Wilminstone in 1888. He had bought the farm from William Stevens, a cattle dealer in Tavistock, although a small part of it was still tenanted by Henry Reddicliffe and later by Walter Reddicliffe. George Henry was born in 1845 and married Theresa Palmer in 1892. They had six children, including Cyril George who continued to farm at Lower Godsworthy. In 1870, however, the Radcliffe family who owned some of Higher Godsworthy had sold the land previously occupied by James Arthur to a Richard Abell of Thrushelton. This man seems to have been related to George Henry Abel (note, one l) although it is not clear how. Richard Abell's son, Thomas Henry Abel (note, now only one l), came into the land on his father's death but farmed at Bratton Clovelly. His son, also Thomas, was joint trustee of his father's will with George Henry Abel. George Henry's son Cyril George married Mary Williams; they had two sons, Richard and Cyril Walter, who carried on the farm, and a daughter, Patricia. In the following years Cyril Walter moved to Higher Godsworthy Farm, buying further land from the Reddicliffes, who had originally moved there from Cudlipptown. At the time of writing, Cyril's three sons, Nicholas, Colin and Phillip, work the two farms.

Cyril Walter Abel leads Keith Birch and Harry Williams into the farm, 1943.

Opposite: *George Henry Abel and Theresa Louise (née Palmer).*

Cyril George Abel marries Mary (née Williams). She was always known as Polly.

George Henry Abel and family.
Left to right, back row: *Gladys Louise (married Arthur Alford), Jessie Elizabeth (married William Roskilly), Lily Evelyn, May Emmeline, Frances Mary (married John Maynard Roskilly);* front row: *George Henry Abel. Cyril George Abel is in front with Theresa Louise Abel (née Palmer).*

The Bellamy family in the courtyard of Coxtor Farm, 1928. Left to right: Francis Edward Bellamy, Sarah Jane and William Bellamy (Francis' father and mother) and Jessie Bellamy. On grandfather's lap is Russell Perkin, son of Francis' sister, Winifred.

Jessie Bellamy, Francis' wife, January 2002.

Bellamy family. Left to right, back row: *Jessie Bellamy (née Rich), Bill, Bryan, Betty (now Gilbert), Francis Bellamy;* front row: *Roger, Ruth, John.*

Left to right: *Ellen Edwards, Elsie Collins, Frank Collins, William Williams. A rare picture of the old miller who was Parish Clerk for 30 years from 1902.*

Ann and Frank Collins at the Mill, 2000.

The Edwards family. Wheelwrights outside Sunnyside at the end of the nineteenth century. Note the circular pattern for making wheels in front of them. William William's daughter Ellen married William Edwards and emigrated to the USA. They had two daughters: Elsie, who married into the Collins family, and Dorothy, who married into the Maunder family.

Marriage of William Roskilly and Jessie Abel.
Left to right, back row: *Mrs Violet Lester,*
Revd Austin Lester, Arthur Alford, Gladys Abel,
George Abel; centre row: *Mrs Ellen Roskilly,*
Joyce Roskilly, William Roskilly, Jessie Abel,
Kathleen Roskilly, Theresa Louise Abel;
front row: *Jean Gloyn and Lucy Perkins.*

Left: *Simmons family, 1950s. Randolph*
and Kathleen (née Roskilly) with their two
daughters, Rosemary (left) *and Valerie* (right).

Bellamy

William Bellamy, born in Hatherleigh in 1836, came to Wedlake as hind for the Mudge family of Collaton in the middle of the nineteenth century. William junr, one of his 11 children, was born in 1865 and continued farming at Wedlake until his death in 1944. Meanwhile, with his son Francis (born in 1902), he had bought Wedlake Farm in 1919. The Doidge family who had been tenants of the Radcliffes' Derriford estate farmed Coppithorne. When Coxtor came on the market in 1948 Francis bought both farms with his son, another William (known as Bill), who has farmed there with his family ever since. Bill married Enid in 1957 and they farmed Coxtor until they retired. In 2002 they still live close at hand but the farm is run by their eldest son Roger. Their second son, Edward, farms at Headlands.

Francis' sister Jessie lived with her father and mother at Lucy Cottage in the village for many years. She was heavily involved in village affairs and was a churchwarden for 38 years. When her parents died she left Lucy Cottage to marry James 'Jim' Cole and lived at Moorview, Cudlipptown. Francis' wife Jessie continues to live close at hand in Coppithorne. Harold, a brother of Francis, was father of Arthur who farmed at Grendon just outside the parish. Arthur's sister Rachel married Edward Mudge to farm at Cholwich Town. Bill's sister Elizabeth, known as Betty, married Robert Gilbert and lives at Pitland Farm, again on the borders of the parish. Betty's daughter, Alison Bullock, has returned to live at Lucy Cottage in the village, completing a full circle. Meanwhile, Bill's brother John continues to farm and run a training agency at Paisley Mead.

Williams

Members of the Williams family are amongst those that have lived longest in the village. It has been possible to trace the family, from church records and family documents, to Richard Williams who died in 1775. His son, also Richard, was responsible for the music in the church before the days of organs. He played the flute with George Mudge on the hautboy, an early type of oboe, and Edward Burley on the violin. Two other unnamed persons in the records of 1791 completed the quintet. At the turn of the century his son took over the office of Parish Clerk from William Burley and held it until 1812. It was the fourth Richard Williams who, whilst working for the Holmes family of Huntingdon, learnt his trade as a miller and took over the tenancy of Higher Mill in 1840 when the Revd Edward Bray had the house and mill rebuilt. His descendants have been there ever since.

The fourth Richard married Harriet Stacey in 1836, whose parents lived in one of the cottages opposite the inn not far from Richard's family, who at the time lived in a cottage near to where Gatehouse Farm is now. Their eldest son John, known as Jack, was a shoemaker and lived in the house now called Midhurst, but for many years it was called Elizabeth Cottage after his wife. Another son called William followed him as a miller and married Elizabeth Ann Bray; he later guided the parish through the changes from being a church parish to a civil parish in 1896. Between 1896 and 1902 he served on the Civil Council as a councillor and then in 1902, when John Holmes who had been appointed Clerk to the Civil Authority in 1896 resigned, William Williams took over and served for 30 years.

It was Ellen, one of William Williams' daughters, whose daughter Elsie married into the Collins family who in 2002 live at Higher Mill, completing occupancy of over 160 years.

Roskilly

Thomas Roskilly of Town Lake, Sydenham Damerel, married Grace Maynard of Cutcrew, Menheniot, Cornwall in the late 1790s. They moved to Willsworthy where their son John Maynard Roskilly was born in 1800. He married Sarah Wilcocks early in 1834 and continued with his father's farm at Willsworthy. In 1847 their son Thomas was born. He married his first cousin, Ellen Maynard Roskilly, who was the daughter of Thomas and Jane Roskilly, living at Pittescombe, Lamerton. It was their son John Maynard Roskilly who married Frances Abel of Godsworthy. The Roskillys acquired Nutley as tenants of the Duke of Bedford at some time in the mid 1800s, and whilst retaining the land at Willsworthy they have lived at Nutley ever since. Thomas Roskilly bought Nutley from the Duke in the early 1900s. John Maynard Roskilly's son, Francis John (Jack), married Winifred Bray and together with their son Thomas (Tom) farmed at Nutley and Willsworthy. Jack's sister Kathleen married Randolph Simmons who farmed at Langsford, Peter Tavy from 1948–88. Kathleen has been the organist at St Peter's since the early 1970s, when Miss Hosking retired, and at the time of writing continues to play regularly for Sunday services.

Dodd

The first of the Dodd family to come to Peter Tavy was John who lived at Coombepark Cottages, now completely derelict, and he married Elizabeth Fuge in 1802. They had 11 children, one of whom was named Edward and had a son called William, who moved away to Sampford Spiney where he married Ann Bray. Their son was also called Edward and he took up work in Whitchurch, but came back to Peter Tavy to live at a house called The Green around 1885. This house forms the centre part of the building we now call Chubb Farm. He married Harriet Freemantle and settled down to develop the farm, which his son, William Frederick, grandson William Edward (Bill) and great grandson Edward Dodd have farmed ever since.

*The marriage of Randolph William Simmons of Ottery Park, Tavistock and Kathleen Roskilly of Nutley.
Left to right, back row: Henry Gribble, Maurice Coumbe, George Abel, Arthur Alford, Gladys Alford,
Harry Mantel, Winifred Bray, William Simmons; centre row: George Uglow, Vera Uglow, Nellie Uglow,
Jennie Daw, Harold Hoyle, Mabel Hoyle, Dorothy Simmons, Francis John Roskilly, Randolph and Kathleen
Simmons, Lucy Mantel, Hetty Mantel, May Gloyn, Marion Perkins, Arthur Perkins, Kitty Bunsell;
seated: Bessie Gribble, Amos Gribble, Mary Simmons, Herbert Simmons, Lilian Simmons,
Frances Roskilly, John Maynard Roskilly, Revd B.C.C. Pratt, Joyce Roskilly and Lily Hearn.*

Thomas Roskilly, who married his cousin, Ellen Maynard Roskilly, from Lamerton. They lived at Nutley.

The Roskilly family at Nutley, 1930s. Left to right: *Francis John, Kathleen, Joyce, Thomas Maynard Roskilly;* parents in front, sitting: *John Maynard Roskilly and Frances Mary (née Abel).*

The Dodd family. Left to right, back row:
William Frederick Dodd and Loftus Edward Dodd.
Their parents, Harriet and Edward Dodd,
are in front.

William F. Dodd with his daughter, Phyllis, and
grandchildren, Peter, Edward and David.

The Dodd family at the seaside. Left to right, back row: Rose Dodd, Harriet Dodd (mother of
Loftus and William) and John Palmer; front row: William Frederick Dodd, William John Dodd
(Empee, son of William Jordan Dodd) and Loftus Edward Dodd.

Another son of that first John Dodd, also called John, had a son William Jordan Dodd who married Elizabeth Fuge, daughter of William and Ann Fuge of Mill Cottages. He was a miner who went to America and returned to buy Southditch, a farm with some nine acres of land at that time. During the early 1890s they moved to Wisdom and took over the Post Office from Elias Bray. At the turn of the century they moved once again to set up a shop and Post Office in an annexe to the house we now call the Old Post Office. Jordan Dodd died in 1906 but his wife and daughter Norah carried on with the shop until 1927 when Elizabeth died. Norah followed her in 1930, but her sister Edith Lane took over and ran the shop until 1965.

William Jordan had a son William John, known as 'Empee', who married Louisa, known as 'Lucy', a daughter of William Williams the miller. They lived in Coombe Cottages, but after he died in 1947 Lucy returned to live at Higher Mill with Frank and Ann Collins.

Collins & Palmer

William Palmer was born at Wapsworthy in 1769 and married a cousin, Anna Maria (née Palmer), when he moved to Radge Farm in around 1810. Among their nine children they had a daughter, also called Anna Maria, who married John Collins. Their son was William Palmer Collins who lived at Tavy House, Mary Tavy and later at Sunnycote, both of which he re-designed and rebuilt. He married Florence Ripley and they had four sons, one of whom was Frank Ripley Collins who married Elsie Edwards, daughter of Henry Edwards, blacksmith and wheelwright at the forge at Sunnyside, Peter Tavy and a granddaughter of William Williams the miller. They were the parents of Frank Collins of Higher Mill.

One of William Palmer's sons relates that in April 1843:

William (Bill) Dodd.

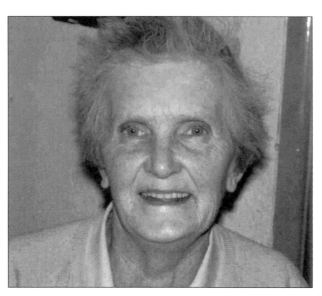
Ivy Dodd, Bill's wife and mother of Peter, David and Edward.

... a monstrous Newfoundland dog was shot in the forest of Dartmoor near Tavy Cleave. He was shot at by several and wounded in many places before he fell. He had made great havoc in the flocks by killing great numbers and suck-ing their blood...

May it not be that Conan Doyle's *'Hound of the Baskervilles'* was inspired by this incident?

By another line, Ellen Garland Bray, a daughter of Thomas Garland Bray of Gatehouse and later Wisdom Farm, married Thomas Collins who lived at Blackdown. He was a schoolmaster and after their marriage they moved to Redruth where they had five boys. This family was responsible for the stained-glass win-dow in Ellen's memory in the church at Peter Tavy. Thomas Collins appears to be a brother of the John Collins who married Anna Maria Palmer and was a mine captain. He is believed to have worked at Rattlebrook Mine.

Vogwill

John Vogwill came to Peter Tavy from Widecombe-in-the-Moor at the time of his first marriage to Joan Dobson, c.1805. He was working at Lower Godsworthy where he farmed before mov-ing to Lower Grimstone Farm, Whitchurch. His wife Joan died in 1818, but he remarried to Patience Martin in 1820. Their daughter Elizabeth married Thomas Holmes from Huntingdon Farm. A son called George married Hannah (née Lang) and lived in Lang Cottage, now Spring House. They had seven children, four of whom stayed in Peter Tavy.

Their eldest son, George Lang Vogwill, who was the village mason, married Elizabeth Job Wright from the village. They had six children. The eldest, Hannah, married Thomas Ash from Tavistock, while Bessie Maria married a Glover and left for Australia. John, the eldest son, married a local girl, Emmie Holmes, and farmed in the area. John represented Peter Tavy on Tavistock Rural District Council for

Above: *John Collins and Anna Maria (née Palmer), c.1880. Their son rebuilt Tavy House, and Sunnycote in Mary Tavy.*

Right: *Elizabeth Job Vogwill (née Wright) with her sister, Polly Weeks (née Wright), outside Brook Cottage. Polly ran one of the village shops.*

The Palmer family living at Radge made up a Church Band for special occasions. This photograph, taken c.1880, would have been after a small, single, manual organ had been installed in the church, and the gallery where they played removed.

many years, and his wife was the church organist. His brother, Thomas, also married a Peter Tavy girl, Lily Cole. He worked in the gold mines in Brazil and West Africa before returning to the old family home at Shula. He managed this smallholding until 1937 when he moved to Hillside, one of the bungalows built by his father-in-law, William Cole, at Langsford. His brother Harold married Joyce Collins from Mary Tavy and farmed at Sampford Spiney before retiring to live at Brook Cottage in Peter Tavy. The youngest brother, Bertie, in common with so many others, died in childhood.

Thomas (Tom) Vogwill in his Special Police uniform during the Second World War.

Rice

Thomas Risse, who lived from 1669–1737, was the first Rice to come to Peter Tavy from Sourton where his father Roger and mother Margritt were living. Four generations were to farm either at Willsworthy, Lanehead or Hilltown. Thomas' great-great-grandson William was born in 1808 and lived at Lanehead, but after a period as a miner at Wheal Betsy he took over the farm at Willsworthy. His son John, born in 1847, worked for his father for a while, then he went to Lower Creason in Mary Tavy before returning to farm at Broadmoor. One of his eight children, Thomas, born in 1883, married Nellie Davey of

Harold Vogwill.

Willsworthy and they lived in the village at Rose Cottage. Thomas worked at Pitts Cleave where he was killed in an accident in 1921. His brother John had meanwhile taken over the farm at Broadmoor. Thomas' son Cecil, better known as 'Bungay', worked at Pitts Cleave for most of his life and married Violet (née Lane), the daughter of George Lane and Edith Jane (née Dodd), who was to run the Post Office when her sister died in 1930. Cecil and Violet's son Michael now lives in Australia, having left the country in 1951.

Mudge

Elizabeth was the earliest known member of the Mudge family to be born to Gregory and Mary Mudge in November 1676 at Willsworthy. The present Mudge family of Collaton and Sowtontown are descended from Roger, one of the 11 children of John Mudge, who married Elizabeth Bloye in 1720. Most of John and Elizabeth's descendants were farm labourers and miners, most of whom stayed around Peter Tavy, marrying into local families. At least 38 different families have been identified, including Arthur, Bellamy, Chubb, Cole, Date, Doidge, Gloyn, Harvie, Holmes and Perkins. Some, but only a few, ventured further afield to the mines at Millom in Yorkshire, others to the Bruce minefields in Ontario, Canada and others again to Australia.

William Mudge came to Sowtontown at the age of two in 1845. His son William was to marry Matilda Rowse Harvie. When they celebrated their Golden Wedding anniversary his advice for a happy marriage was 'work together; exercise the principle of give and take'. Sowtontown at that time belonged to the Radcliffe estate but was bought from them by the Mudges in the 1950s, where they stayed until the late 1970s.

George Mudge, born in 1826, came to Higher Collaton at much the same time as William took over from the Cole family at Sowtontown. One of his grandchildren, also a George, died in the First World War and is remembered on the memorial in the churchyard at Peter Tavy. Collaton is still the home of George and Charles Mudge and their families, completing five successive generations who have farmed there.

The Peter Tavy Inn, 1948. 'Bungay' Rice stands in front. Bungay, or Bungee as his son tells us he was known, worked at Pitts Cleave and lived in the village. He was a big man and held the records at the quarry for many years for individually quarrying the most rock.

The Mudge family of Sowtontown, 1930s. Left to right, back row: *Martha who married William Lethbridge, Edna who married James Perkins, John who married Joyce Miles and Mary who married Arthur Bellamy of Grendon;* centre row: *Annie who married Cecil Cole, Matilda (née Harvie), William Mudge and George who married Barbara Eggins;* front row: *William who died young, Nancy who married Arthur Dingle.*

Mills & Milling

Higher Mill

In 1379 Walter Dymok was living in Peter Tavy and may have been the local miller. In 1409 Elizabeth Dymok, who was the widow of Walter and had been one of the early Members of Parliament for Tavistock in 1406, left the mill at Peter Tavy to her son John. Over 250 years later the inheritance of the six daughters of Francis Glanville of Kilworthy, who died in 1668, included a dwelling house, grist mill and garden in Peter Tavy. Margaret, one of Francis Glanville's daughters, transferred the corn and grist mill at Peter Tavy, which was then in the tenancy of William Barrett, to the Rolle family in 1674. She also gave the Rolles much other land. Contemporary correspondence in the church records suggests that Barrett's tenancy was at Higher Mill.

In 1740 the Kinsman family bought the mill from the Rolle family and leased it to the Blachford family for short periods in 1745 and again in 1761. Thereafter, the Kinsmans retained the mill until they sold it in 1806 to Edward Bray. On his death it was inherited by Edward's son, Revd E.A. Bray, Vicar of Tavistock, in whose family it remained well into the twentieth century.

Peter Holmes, a farmer at Huntingdon Farm, held the lease at the mill in 1788 and his family retained their position as millers until 1840. Eliza Bray in her book *Rural Scenes*, published around 1840, describes how:

The Mill had been drawn and painted over and over again... and was never yet unsold on the hands of the artist. The subject it affords is strikingly characteristic. A rush of water turns the wheel, and forms a cascade that falls into a rapid mountain stream as clear as the brightest crystal; the thatched gable of the Mill is covered with ivy; a little bridge crosses the stream opposite the cottage door... Near the Mill cottage the children assemble in groups; and ponies, donkies, pigs and cocks and hens, are all found there, forming the most animated accompaniments that a Morland or a Wilkie would have desired to complete the picture of rustic life.

Higher Mill, 1905. At this stage the mill was still working and corn would be brought and raised to the dormer on the left side of the picture. The water-wheel is out of sight, but the machinery inside the door would grind the corn and it could be returned in sacks. Note the pigeon nesting boxes on the wall above the door. The part of the house covered in ivy was where William Williams, the miller, lived with his family.

This etching was done before 1800 and shows the water-wheel of the old thatched mill. Artistic licence has allowed the brook to run rather close to the mill; it should have passed to the right of the building in the back of the picture. The small bridge that can be seen in later pictures was not built until the mid 1800s and access to the mill was via a shallow ford. The wall of the shippen is shown on the right of the picture and remains there today, adjacent to the Causeway along which the people are walking from the village.

A painting from before 1840. The mill was rebuilt when the thatched roof was removed. Mrs Bray, whose husband owned the mill, was not too pleased by the appearance of the new building.

One of the grinding stones used at Higher Mill. It now stands outside the old millhouse.

Nevertheless, a surveyor of the mill in 1835 reports that it is 'so much in a dilapidated condition I shall not attempt to particularise.' Revd Bray decided that the mill should be rebuilt and the thatch, much admired by artists, was replaced by slate. This work was not completed until 1840 when Richard Williams, by whose family the mill is still occupied at the time of writing, took over. Richard died in 1880 and his son William Williams became the miller.

The fields of Peter Tavy farms were turning from corn to pasture because imported wheat from America was lowering the price of that crop, and the need for a mill receded. Lower Mill had ceased working before the First World War and Higher Mill followed in the early years of the 1920s. The water-wheel that drew so much attention and required so much upkeep no longer exists, and the leat, stretching from the Coombe Clam to the mill itself, is still running when the brook is high. Water for the other mills is taken from the brook below Higher Mill and runs in a similar fashion north of the Garage to serve Gatehouse before it turns in a sharp right angle to descend to Lower Mill.

The balance of village life was a delicate one. Arthur Bellamy recounted how George Abel had told him how they took their corn to Lower Mill for grinding, but bought any corn or flour they wanted from William Williams at Higher Mill. One of the requisites of anyone taking corn to be ground was a 'cat' – a fine muslin bag in which fine dust and barley could be caught during the grinding process – which would be taken back home to make bread.

The wooden cogs of the main gearing at Higher Mill with some of the tools found close by.

Higher Mill in 1984. The bridge seen in the forefront of the picture was built by a subscription collected by William Williams at the end of the nineteenth century, after floods had washed down large rocks from the moor and blocked access to the lane on the right, which leads to the Coombe.

A drawing of a young Eliza Bray in the early-nineteenth century.

The estimated cost of repairing the water-wheel at Higher Mill in 1850. Details are provided for the wood types to be used for different parts of the wheel. The water-wheel was 14 feet in diameter and endured a great deal of heavy usage. These repairs were required just ten years after a complete renovation and only lasted until 1863, when a new wheel, except for the axle, was required.

Lower Mill

The resurgence of agriculture after the Commonwealth years (1649–60), together with the high price of corn, may have been the pressures that brought Lower Mill into existence in around 1670. Walter Eastlake seems to have been the first miller, to be followed into the profession by his widow only a few years later. In 1780 the miller was a John Page, a tenant of Sarah Parsons who was the owner of Langsford Farm and other land in the area, but within 20 years, by marriage or purchase, the Roskilly family were the owners. They did not work the mill themselves and a series of tenants included Thomas Blatchford, who by 1810 was the miller at Higher Mill, and Roger Holmes, whose family also held the tenancy of Higher Mill at the time. In a marriage settlement during 1834, between Frances Roskilly and

Daniel Perkin, the trustees were Thomas Roskilly and John Physick. It was agreed that the property would revert to Thomas Roskilly should Daniel and Frances die without children. Over the next 30 years numerous millers worked the mill, including John Date, Samuel Quick, Robert Down, Isaac Dawe, George Vogwill and John Jones. The mill, having apparently reverted to the Roskilly family, was now owned by Miss Roskilly. For the next 20 years the Gibbings father and son, Richard and Gregory, worked the mill in conjunction with a smallholding of about four acres. But at the turn of the century two local farmers, Charles Doidge of Coxtor and George Abel of Godsworthy, had taken the tenancy. It did not last long and John Sleeman bought the mill from a Roskilly family trust. He was the last to work it for corn and it was closed in 1910.

Gatehouse Mill

Gatehouse Farm was probably built in the period of recovery after the Napoleonic Wars around 1820. A mill with a water-wheel was attached and served by the same leat as Lower Mill from the Colley, or Peter Tavy Brook as it was then known. It does not seem to have been more than a domestic mill to deal with small quantities of corn from the farm and perhaps to grind farm tools as an edge tool mill.

Note: Cudlipptown, Willsworthy and Hillbridge are all reported to have had mills at one time, but little remains of them.

Left: Cecil Cole, at Lower Mill, is standing alongside the gearing below the grindstone.

Postal Services in Peter Tavy

The earliest days of postal deliveries to the village date back to 1637, when letters and parcels came to Peter Tavy from Ashburton where they were transferred from a mail coach to a man on horseback in order to cross the moor. This service seems to have continued until at least 1700 as there are references to the Ashburton post in letters dated in the 1690s. However, in 1669 post for Tavistock was also being received from Plymouth where it had arrived on the Liskeard coach, and by 1697 Tavistock emerged as one of three sub-Post Offices controlled from Okehampton. It was finally given the status of Main Post Office in 1791 under the supervision of Mr Nicholas Hines.

With the arrival of the 'penny post' in 1841 there was a great increase in mail, and smaller offices began to emerge in the villages. The first Post Office came to Peter Tavy in 1860 in the hands of John Garland Bray, who was living at Gatehouse Farm. By 1866 it had moved to Wisdom and was in the control of Elias Bray, where it became the centre for Peter Tavy. It was still just a mail receipt and delivery office and any important Post Office business had to be done at Tavistock. The wall collection boxes were placed at Peter Tavy, Cudlipptown and Willsworthy in 1876 and are still in use today. They were emptied at 5p.m. with letters for delivery arriving from Tavistock by foot post at 7.15a.m. They were sorted in the village and delivered by the Postmaster, although in those days many would have called in to collect and send their post.

By 1892 William Jordan Dodd was living at Wisdom and had taken over the post duties. His family were to be responsible for the postal services in the village for over 70 years. In 1900 they moved to the 'Old Post Office' where they had set up a shop selling general goods and sweets in an annexe to the house. William died in 1906 but his wife Elizabeth continued until her death in 1927. Their daughter, Norah, had helped her mother with the shop and took over after her mother's death, until her own death in 1930. Her sister Edith Lane, known as Nellie, had moved away when she had married and returned to Peter Tavy to take over the shop and Post Office until she retired in 1965. By this time the shop was equipped with a public telephone and provided most of the postal services. Villagers recall how, as children, they would go into Nellie's shop as they sometimes got an extra sweet in the packet if the weight was not 'just right', whereas Polly, down the road, kept a hammer to split a barley stick or toffee to make sure it was a correct measure. Nellie died in 1971.

Below: *The Old Post Office, an annexe to the cottage, is where William Jordan Dodd and his family ran the village Post Office between 1902 and 1965. The tell-tale advert for Lyons tea on the door indicates that it was also one of the village shops.*

Above: *The old shop and Post Office window at Wisdom, through which parcels were handed to customers. Before the Post Office transferred to the Old Post Office in 1902, it was run from Wisdom for nearly 50 years.*

The Mobile Postal Service at station in the village. The Mobile Postal Service was the first in the country and started in Peter Tavy in April 1999. It remains on station in the Square for 30 minutes to do business once a week.

The postman's hut at Cudlipptown Green. This hut was built on Cudlipptown Green in 1899 after permission had been granted by Revd J.E. Kempe, the lord of the manor, for the postman delivering to the hamlets on the moor beyond Cudlipptown to shelter before making the return journey. Each individual postman had to pay a rent of 6d. per year and the lease was determinable by three months' notice on either side. Richard Cruze was the first postman to pay the rental, followed by A.J. (Bert) Jago, shown here at Christmas, 1901. Note the plants around the door.

In the 1930s William John Dodd, William and Elizabeth's son who was known by his nickname 'Empee', delivered the post after it had been sorted in the Post Office, to outlying farms including Twist and Wedlake. Many people in the village recall taking post to the farms for Mrs Lane during the war years, when postmen were in short supply. Amongst these people was Frank Collins at Higher Mill, who combined the milk round with post delivery. Following Mrs Lane's death the Post Office transferred to the cottages opposite Wisdom and was run by Mrs Weeks. It subsequently moved one cottage nearer the chapel, to Jasmine Cottage. Here there was a succession of Postmasters including Bill Bailey, Ruth and Walter Graham, 'Tiny' and Eric Gait, Mick and Joan Harvey, the Pollards, the Stratfords and,

finally, Sylvia and Alan Sankey. Final closure was at Christmas in 1996.

However, the story does not end there. On Thursday 15 April 1999 the first travelling mobile Post Office in the country drew up outside the Village Hall. It remained for 30 minutes to complete the village postal business and moved on to other villages in West Devon and East Cornwall. From the time of the closure of the village Post Office a local councillor William (Bill) Lane had been negotiating with the authorities for such a service and at last with the support of the Rural Development Commission it had come to fruition. The first mobile postal service in the country is now a regular part of village life, handling all the postal services except, of course, the mail for which the postal services were originally set up!

Elizabeth Dodd, wife of William Jordan Dodd, was the first Postmistress in Peter Tavy when she took on the role after her husband's death in 1906. She kept the shop and Post Office in the 'Old Post Office', an annexe to her cottage in the centre of the village, until she died in 1927.

Victorian postboxes at Cudlipptown and Willsworthy. These postboxes were installed in 1876 and are still in use today. The Post Office at Peter Tavy opened every day to receive mail from a man who went out to the boxes in all weathers to clear them every evening and ensure the post left the village at 5p.m. promptly.

Shops of Peter Tavy

In the *Kelly's Directory* of 1850 Samuel Date and William Fuge are both described as shopkeepers, but in the Census of the following year Samuel is noted as a miner and William Fuge as a retired house proprietor. It seems likely that neither was devoted to a shop full time but, like many others in the village, they had two jobs – often their basic living combined with mining or farming. By 1856 Samuel had passed his business on to John Date, and Philip Lamphee had taken over from William Fuge. At this time John Date was the miller at Lower Mill, so it is probable that at least one shop was based at the mill.

village have referred to a small thatched shop near the church and this may have been it.

In 1893 Mrs Jane Wright opened a shop in what is now part of Midhurst Cottage. By 1910 her daughter Mrs Mary Weeks, better known as Polly, had taken it on and she kept it open until the end of the Second World War. By this time she was over 80 years old and reportedly thoroughly fed up with rationing and the coupon systems. She died in 1958 aged 94 years.

The shops were not the only 'retail outlets'. In addition to the farms selling dairy produce and eggs

Polly and Jonathan Weeks outside their shop, c.1910. Jonathan is pictured standing on the cobbled right of way that divided the shop from the garden and Polly is in the shade in her white dress. The pergola was used for anyone wanting temperance refreshment and a rest in the sun.

In the 1866 directories we find John Garland Bray, the same man who had opened the first Post Office in 1860, as shopkeeper and farmer at Gatehouse, and William Rider is described as the village grocer. So it seems to have remained, until James Ware, who had done his stint as landlord of the Inn from 1864 to 1868, took on the role of shopkeeper in 1873, only to pass it to his wife Betsy by 1878. She was to run the store well into the 1890s. It is difficult to identify sites for all of the shops; often they were no more than a room in a house, perhaps only open for limited times on certain days of the week. It seems likely that Betsy Ware had her shop in one of the cottages opposite the inn, alongside the smithy and near the church. Older members of the

from their doors, there were visiting traders such as the fish sellers. James Perkins recalled Harry Selleck who lived in Coombe Cottages and used to sell oil, soap and brushes from his 'jingle'.

Meanwhile, William Jordan Dodd had moved the Post Office from Wisdom to an annexe alongside his cottage and his wife Elizabeth started to sell sweets and groceries. The shop at 'Midhurst' returned to Lower Mill where Mrs Maud Moyse was living with her daughters Olive and Lily, who took the work on until 1965. Bill and Lily Bailey opened their new shop at Jasmine Cottage in 1965 when the shop at the Old Post Office closed and Nellie Lane retired. Some villagers remember how the goods were at first displayed all over the furniture of the sitting room with

Right: *Maud Moyse (née Walter) was born in Brentor and had six brothers. At 93 years of age she could still recall poetry she had learnt as a child. A particular couplet always stood out in her memory:*

'Though poor they were, too proud to beg, too upright for to steal,
But gladly would they sweep and clean to gain an honest meal.'

She went into service at the age of 14, earning 2 shillings a week. By the age of 25 she was a cook in a private house in Tavistock, earning £20 a year, and she married and came to live in Peter Tavy. Her husband, Bert, was killed in a quarry accident at Pitts Cleave. They had two daughters, Olive and Lily, and Maud ran the shop at Lower Mill with their help after her husband died in 1942 until about 1965. She died at the age of 94 in 1987.

Top right: *Nellie Lane. When William Jordan Dodd moved the Post Office from Wisdom to the annexe attached to his cottage, his wife Elizabeth started selling groceries and sweets. After his death in 1906 she carried on until her own death in 1927. By this time Nellie (pictured), who had left Peter Tavy when she got married, had returned. When her sister Norah died shortly after her mother, Nellie took over the shop and ran it until 1965. She moved to Village Way and died there in 1971, aged 91 years.*

Above: *Mary (Polly) Weeks. Polly was the daughter of Jane Wright, who had opened the shop in 1893. In 1910 Polly took over from her aging mother, who died in 1913 aged 83 years. Polly had married Jonathan Weeks, a committed Methodist who held 'Temperance' meetings in the village and started the 'Band of Hope'. These were so successful that more than 50 villagers took the 'pledge', and became known as 'The Peter Tavy Blues'.*

Mr and Mrs Graham in the shop, c.1965. They left Peter Tavy to breed Dexter cattle. She won Champion place with Woodtown Polly within a few years.

Mr and Mrs Harvey in the shop, c.1980.

Alan and Sylvia Sankey kept the last general shop and Post Office in Peter Tavy. It closed for the last time at Christmas 1996.

The Shop behind 'Midhurst', 1920. The entrance to the shop was between the two chimneys on the left of the picture. Notice the board on the wall indicating the shop entrance. The half window just visible on Wisdom, the building to the right of the picture, was used to take in letters and other mail when the Post Office was based there.

tables and chairs, and even the piano, being called into use. Ruth Graham was the next to take on the shop but a year or two later Mr Gait came and changed everything. Concerned about a tendency for the Colley Brook to overflow onto the Causeway outside his shop, he started a campaign that led to the clearing of grass and stonework in the lane. It was not until after he left the village that the next flood of the Colley actually entered the shop for the first time. It was after this that the present stone steps in the Causeway were built. Mick and Joan Harvey picked up the pieces, followed by the Pollards and Stratfords with Sylvia and Alan Sankey finally closing the shop at Christmas in 1996.

The Story of Peter Tavy Inn

The early history of the inn is bound up with the village church, St Peter's. The present church has Norman (eleventh-century) connections and required rebuilding in the fourteenth and fifteenth centuries, when a great part of the walls and tower needed to be repaired. In those days, stonemasons moved from village to village to do much of their work and Peter Tavy was no different. To accommodate these workers a cottage was built where they lived until all the work was completed and they moved on to the next job. It is generally believed that the present inn started in just this way, perhaps as far back as 1400 when much church building was being done. What happened to the cottage after the masons left is not known; it is probable that it was absorbed into the village. It could have been no more than a single-storey building, with perhaps a division to make two rooms, and a thatched roof. Later a second storey was added to provide overnight space for weary travellers.

At the entrance gate to the churchyard there are two cottages, known now as Church Cottages. They are also old, having started life in the late-fifteenth century as a brewhouse. This was the site of the annual celebration of the Feast of St Peter on 29 June and other feasts of the Church calendar. It also served to provide a meeting-place for people after the service and somewhere they could stable a horse for the return journey to their farms. In winter they could keep in the warm. These brewhouses, or church houses as they became known, are found near most ancient churches in Devon. They also served to accommodate poor travellers who could not pay to stay at the inn. It did not belong to the church but was held in common from the lord of the manor by the churchwardens. The brewing of ale was a prerogative of the lord of the manor but usually vested in the churchwardens and incumbent. After 1495 all brewing had to be controlled by the Justice of the Peace (magistrate). In 1552 licensing of the sale of liquor had commenced and the price had gone up; in 1550 the cost of a gallon of ale had risen to 2 pennies; at the start of the century a penny had bought two gallons of ale!

In 1723 the incumbent, Revd John Gilbert later to become Archbishop of York, rebuilt the rectory in the

The Peter Tavy Inn, 1930. Note the wall in front of the inn, with the gate just beyond the car.
The area this side of the wall would have been space for horses when, earlier in the century,
they came to the blacksmith's forge opposite the inn.

The Peter Tavy Inn, 2000. The land in front of the inn has been cleared, forming a small staff car park
and a raised beer garden; a larger car park at the back of the inn now serves customers.

village and with it a brewhouse, thus depriving the church house of its direct source of ale. It seems probable that this led to the villagers seeking another means of slaking their thirst and what place was more convenient than the house down the road, owned by the parish and no longer used for watch-keeping. It is also probable, although no record has yet been found which verifies this, that by this time there was a need for a parish poorhouse for those in the parish who had fallen on hard times and had nowhere to live.

The Peter Tavy Inn, except for a short period in the 1950s, has always been a free house and until the major alterations were done in 1988–89 it was certainly only a small building. Described in a sale catalogue of 1819 it comprised a kitchen, bar, parlour, three lodging rooms and a stable. It is probable that the landlord and his family lived across the yard in one of the cottages, then known as Churchtown Cottages, of which now only Meadowside remains. In the period of 1889 to 1900 when the Prout family, and then the Edwards family, lived at the inn and the cottage opposite, they traded as blacksmiths. This seems to have ceased when William and Mary Salter took over in 1901. William and Mary had come from Newton Abbot to take on the inn but William was found drowned in April of that same year. He had apparently fallen into the Tavy whilst trying to reach Tavistock for a doctor to attend his daughter who was in labour. Mary carried on at the inn until 1907 and later died at the age of 61 years in 1910.

In 1819 the pub was owned by the Sleeman family and on the death of William Sleeman the estate, which included a share in the inn at Peter Tavy, was sold. Prudence Stephens had previously held a licence at the inn and bought a half share.

Mary White owned the inn between 1854 and 1875 when an S. Lewis bought it, but by 1926 the ownership was with Charles Seymour, who retained it until 1946. At this date the Plymouth Brewery, who sold it back into private ownership around 1964, bought the inn. Since that time succeeding owners have also been the landlords of the inn.

Mary Warne recalls that in 1926, during her childhood, when her father Syd Thomas was land-lord, the inn consisted of a living room immediately inside the front door, which had a kitchen range. To the right of the living room was a kitchen, which was also used for storage and general purposes. It had a very high ceiling and the walls were limewashed with the help of a stirrup pump. To the left of the front door was the bar, which had no counter. On the right wall of the bar was a fireplace, two or three set-tles and a trestle table. The end wall was complete, except for a doorway in the right-hand corner that opened into the cellar. Beyond the cellar was a small room that was approached from the courtyard and was used for afternoon teas and other meals if they had people staying in the guest room. Beer (mild ale

and ale) was served at a trestle table. There was no barmaid and usually someone would come from the kitchen to serve the beer, leaving the customers to call if they required more. In the evenings the landlord would perhaps stay in the bar for a general chat and be available to serve the beer. He would probably have been at work elsewhere, perhaps mining, dur-ing the day. There would be no women in the pub unless they were staying as guests.

Upstairs there was a large room used every Thursday evening for the meetings of the local Lodge of the Antedeluvian Order of the Buffalo. Mary Warne's father had been a long-term member and used to go to the meetings when they were held in Tavistock. When he took the licence at Peter Tavy Inn the meetings moved there, with many members coming long distances to participate.

The inn gained a moment of fame when it served as a location for the feature film *Run Wild, Run Free*, featuring Sir John Mills, and several villagers appeared as 'extras' in the background of scenes shot there.

It was not until 1994 that a full renovation of the building was undertaken, providing separate accom-modation for the owner and any guests. It was the first time that the inn had been closed since the First World War, at which time the Band of Hope was strong in Peter Tavy as in many places around the country. In 1916 King George V vowed that he would take no more alcohol until the end of the war. It had a startling effect in this village. The inn had not been doing well and an application was submit-ted to Tavistock Court to close it down completely. Whether by luck or providence the application was not completed in time for the relevant sitting so it was delayed until the next sitting, by which time it had been withdrawn. However, the inn was not very successful and finally closed for several months, reopening in time to renew the annual licence!

During building work in 1988 outhouses and a toilet block were converted into a kitchen and beer cellar. An extension at the back of the old house was built to provide restaurant space, with an additional storey providing living accommodation above. The partition at the end of the bar was opened to give access to the small tearoom and the original doorway closed. A serving counter opened up the old beer cellar to the bar. It was not until the mid 1990s that the bar moved from the room on the left of the entrance to its present position at the front of the inn.

Some interesting features still remain. The front door retains a sixteenth-century lock and behind the present bar the remnants of the granite mantle and the old kitchen fireplace are clearly seen. Many of the distressed and irregular timbers are the result of the clever use of recycled timber from local barns, replac-ing those that had rotted with age. The settle in the bar is a restoration made from the floorboards of a local disused chapel. A watchkeeper's window still

Publicans at the Peter Tavy Inn

1813	Prudence STEPHENS
1819	James COWLING
1821	Prudence STEPHENS
1822	John and Sarah COX
1823	Mark and Sally RICKARD
1835	Thomas WARE
1864	James WARE (Thomas' son)
1868	William SUSSEX
1878	William MILMAN
1883	William HANKE
1890	Robert and Mary PROUT
1893	Annie PROUT (Robert and Mary's daughter)
1896	James MELLERS
1897	William DYMOND
1901	William and Mary SALTER
1907	James RICE
1914	Aubrey GREGORY

Closed for short period at end of the First World War, when an application was made to withdraw the licence.

1919	Florence PENROSE
1923	Charles SEYMOUR (still the owner in 1951)
1926	Albert MAUNDER (for about a month)
1926–40	Sydney Peter THOMAS
1940–46	Edith THOMAS (Sydney's wife)
1946–51	William W. and Mary WARNE (Mary is Edith and Sydney Thomas' daughter)
1951	? PAYNE

About this time it was bought by Plymouth Breweries, who sold to Symonds Breweries in around 1970, which was bought up by Courage Breweries, and in turn it was sold to the Somervilles in 1982.

1958–60	Paddy MILES
1960	Peggy BRAZIERS
1964–65	Harry NOCK
1965–72	Bob ROBERTS
1972–82	Anna and David LIGHTFOOT
1982–84	Paul and Linda SOMERVILLE
1984–92	Janice and Phil HAWKINS
1992–94	John and Gill DIPROSE
1994–98	John VAUGHAN and Rita WESTLAKE
1998–	Graeme and Karen SIM

exists in the private apartments facing Brentor where, at the time of the Spanish Armada (1588), the watchkeeper would warn the villagers if a beacon were lit and then light another beacon on Smeardon to pass on the message of the threatened invasion.

The true story about 'mad Mitch', otherwise known as Frank Mitchell, a notorious criminal of the 1950s and '60s, may never be known. His association with the Peter Tavy Inn is based upon reports that during his stay on Dartmoor, from 1962 until his escape in 1966, he behaved well enough to be given the privilege of working outside the prison at Baggator in an 'Honour party'. It was mid 1965 when he would, as one prison warder has put it, 'disappear into the mist in the morning and reappear at night'. It is said that he had found himself a local girlfriend and used to meet her at the inn. Joan Amos, who worked for Bob Roberts the landlord, recalled how Mitchell bought tobacco and chocolates at the inn. He sold the tobacco when he got back to the prison but would give the sweets and chocolate to children he met on his wanderings. She also remembered an occasion when two men, whom she later recognised as the Kray twins, came to the Inn asking for Mitchell. The evidence that he came there lay in an old small kit bag Mitchell carried, which was supposed to have been left behind on the last occasion he visited. The kit bag has since disappeared. In December 1966 the Kray brothers assisted Mitchell's escape and he was murdered a matter of days later.

The Peter Tavy Inn, 1961.
Left to right: *Dave Williams, ?, Jack Bowhay, Sid Warren, Rose Warren;* front right: *Frank Cooper, Arthur Ball.*

Peter Tavy Garage

A group stands on the bridge to survey the new garage, 1925. Note that an extension has been added to the back of the building at a later date.

Leonard Cole tries the spanners outside his father's garage. The petrol pump was still in use and the motorists' shop can be seen behind the car.

Max Allen and Trevor Cudmore outside the garage; don't be put off by the telephone number – the exchange for the district was at Mary Tavy.

The garage, 1984. The petrol pump, which can just be seen at the front of the garage, was still there at the time of writing.

Bert Cole built the garage at Peter Tavy to house his newly-acquired charabanc during 1925. The site, between the Colley Brook and a leat serving Lower Mill and Gatehouse, had previously been open ground which was used as gardens by the tenants of the immediate cottages. Bert was also interested in developing his motor engineering services and arranged to have a service pit within the garage and a petrol pump. The pump is still there at the time of writing, but the shop in which he kept his oil and car polishes, that can be seen in the photograph, has long since disappeared. As his business increased he bought another charabanc. Access must have been awkward because, as the photo shows, the only entrance was from the opening to the right of way

behind the cottages, which also served Pollie Weeks' shop and the village well. In 1953, when Pridhams took over the bus service, they were using larger buses and the wall was knocked down to provide turning space.

Heinz Pinge bought the property from Pridhams at some time during the 1960s. He proposed to build a flat at the back of the garage in which he would live, but was refused planning permission. The building was later leased to a Mr Hanson who used it as a workshop for preparing theatrical properties and stage sets. Then around 1980 Max Allen took out a lease for a motor engineering garage as Bert Cole had originally set up 60 years earlier. Max Allen has been there ever since.

Public Transport

Bert Cole's first charabanc.

The earliest motor bus service to the village was started soon after the First World War by the Devon Motor Transport Company. A bus that ran between Okehampton and Tavistock on Fridays (market day) came back to Peter Tavy to pick up villagers at 10.15 in the morning and would return in the afternoon, leaving the New Market Hotel in Tavistock at 4p.m. The fare was a shilling each way. This service was withdrawn in 1923, whether from lack of support or because more profitable journeys were found is not known.

Bertram (Bert) Cole, who lived at Elizabeth Cottage (now Midhurst) and ran a small motor repair garage in the village, took up the challenge of providing some form of transport for the people of Peter

Tavy. In the early months of 1924 an announcement appeared saying that he would run a car and lorry service which would take passengers to and from Tavistock on market days, at a fare of a shilling return and ninepence for a single ticket. For these runs the lorry was fitted with bench seats for passengers and goods were also carried. A car was available for any overflow and also provided a taxi service.

The venture seems to have been successful as the following year he bought a second-hand Crossley charabanc with 14 seats to provide the service. This released his truck and a five-seater car for private parties and removals. His venture seems to have been burgeoning as between 1923 and 1925 he built the garage we see today, with a pit and facilities for

The Eddystone Belle.

Bert Cole's advert in the local paper, 1925.

Bert Cole's last coach.

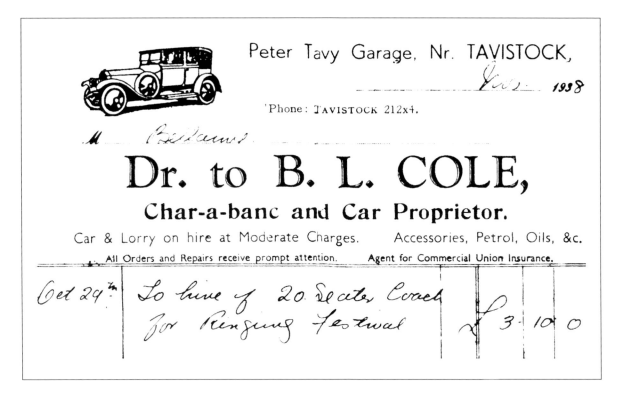

A bill made out to J.C. Bellamy, Captain of the Tower, for a 20-seater coach for the bell-ringing festival, 1938.

servicing not only his own vehicles but those of other villagers, farmers or passing motorists, and he installed the first and only petrol pump. On its side the charabanc carried the name 'Eddystone Belle', perhaps a simple addition to the name of the previous owners of the bus, Eddystone Motor Services, whose own buses were marked simply with the word Eddystone.

Over the next ten years Bert Cole developed his market-day service with buses to and from Cudlipptown and Wapsworthy, and another incorporating Moortown and Moorshop, reaching Tavistock by the Princetown road. The buses left the village at 8.45a.m. and 10.30a.m. with the return journey at 2.30p.m. and 4.00p.m.

In 1929 the old charabanc was replaced with a new 14-seater Chevrolet, painted in blue and called the 'Peter Tavy Blue' (Bus Service). In 1939 some of the services had to be reduced; buses to and from Cudlipptown and Wapsworthy were stopped and some of the market-day services operated only in the summer months. In the same year the Chevrolet was sold and a larger 20-seater Bedford was bought, enabling him to accept contracts to carry servicemen in the local camps at Pitts Cleave and Plaister Down which were set up during the war.

Meanwhile, fuel rationing and low numbers of car owners maintained a steady flow of private hire work with the taxi, the charabanc and the heavy haulage lorry being in demand. After the Second World War the restructuring of the education system led to the senior pupils being transferred to Tavistock from Peter Tavy School, and transport had to be provided by Devon County Council. Bert Cole tendered for the contract and was successful. He was paid £1.10s. a day for his coach to collect and return the children each morning and afternoon in the school term.

In 1947 Bert Cole bought a second charabanc, this time able to accommodate 30 people, but he was finding his commitments too great and decided to sell all but the school contracts to White and Goodman. In 1948, although still working for them, he sold them the remaining contracts. These contracts were just what Gilbert White had wanted to enable his firm to develop. The new service, known as 'Sunshine Coaches', provided the Peter Tavy service for up to four days a week, but in 1953 White and Goodman passed their holdings to Pridham Brothers of Lamerton.

The excursion programme introduced by Bert Cole some years earlier had been abandoned in 1952 but was now re-introduced. Because of restrictions on picking up passengers, Peter Tavy as the starting point had virtually its own service to the home matches of Plymouth Argyle.

Hillbridge School reopened in 1941 to accommodate the many evacuees that had come to the area, having been closed since 1924. It only remained open until 1946, when, with the war over, the evacuees returned home to the cities. During this period of activity Bert Cole provided a bus service to Willsworthy and Longbettor Gate in the winter, but Syd Thomas from the inn got the contract to convey the schoolchildren. James Perkins recalled his old

The "Peter Tavy Blue" Bus

SERVICES & TIME TABLE
(FRIDAYS ONLY)

TO TAVISTOCK

BUSES WILL LEAVE

Petertavy	*8.45*	*Wapsworthy*	*11.15*
Petertavy	*10.30*	*Cudlipptown*	*11.25*
Petertavy	*3.0*	*Petertavy -*	*11.30*
Moor Town	*9.45*	*Moor Shop -*	*10.0*

BUSES WILL DEPART

FROM TAVISTOCK
FOR

Peter Tavy at 10.15, 10.45, 2.30 & 4.0

Cudlipptown and Wapsworthy at 4.0

Moor Shop and Moor Town at 1.0

Printed by The Tavistock Printers. 7 King Street, Tavistock.

'Peter Tavy Blue' bus service timetable, 1929.

Chrysler which never started properly but still managed to pick up the children from northern areas of the parish, including Hill Bridge and Wapsworthy, and bring them down to the school. In 1947 it was the turn of James Cole of Cudlipptown to collect the children from Willsworthy and bring them to Cudlipptown, where they were transferred to the Peter Tavy coach for the rest of the journey to school. In 1950 a car was provided to bring the children from Cudlipptown, Willsworthy and beyond to Peter Tavy when Bert Cole's bus was not running. With the closure of the school at Peter Tavy in 1959 all the children were transferred to Dolvin Road School. The number of children living outside the village fell and the bus service did not go beyond the garage. Meanwhile, national bus companies have provided a bus service. In the 1950s this service ran around mid morning on four days a week, but this was steadily being withdrawn as the number of people owning motor cars increased. Today the service is restricted to two days a week to include Friday, market day in Tavistock.

Horses, Ponies & Recollections

Before the days of public transport and cars people walked, rode a horse or used a bicycle. Stories of miners leaving Peter Tavy to walk up the Coombe and over Staple Tor to reach work at Merrivale were recounted, along with stories of others, who walked deep into the moor at the start of the week and returned only when work finished the following Saturday. By the end of the nineteenth century the bicycle had been invented and came into common use, followed swiftly by the motorcycle.

Farmers for the most part kept to their horses when working but used a trap or 'jingle' if going to town. Strictly a 'jingle' was a 'governess' car, though from the only pictures we have of local farmers they were using the 'Ralli' car. One such was Johnnie Reep who would recover his horse from Gatehouse after a visit to the inn – luckily from there the horse knew the way home to Gnattor. Another was Johnnie Phillips from Youlditch whose family had farmed there for more than a 150 years. He lived alone after his brother and sister died and was the last to take his trap regularly to market – it was said that the horse knew every stop on the way back home. The story goes that they were a family of few words. When Walter went to fight in the First World War he received only a single letter from home, all the time he was away. It read 'What did you do with the hook before you left?' Another who used his trap regularly was Edward Dodd. He would kill a pig every week and drive to Plymouth to sell the pork. He changed the horse in both directions at Magpie Bridge, Horrabridge. Peggy Stephens' mother, always known for helping anyone who was in need, would drive her pony called 'Ginger' with an open 'jingle' out to Standon, Baggator and Gnattor from her home at Longbettor. The doyen of Peter Tavy, however, was Johnnie Reep who lived at Gnattor. He was always smartly dressed with highly polished gaiters. He was very knowledgeable about stock, in particular about the Dartmoor pony, and traded all over the country, driving to Lydford Station in a meticulously clean and polished 'jingle' to take a train to Scotland for sales.

With cattle and horses all around the village, there were many watering places. Some would water in the Causeway, others in the leat outside Brook Cottage. There was a large granite trough at the top of Langsford Hill where the roads meet, and another at the inn. Cobs were kept for general haulage and were in demand when heavy rocks had to be moved. George Mudge at Collaton developed a general haulage side to his farming and would carry lime from Morwellham for other farmers or builders.

The arrival of the motorbike did not pass Peter Tavy by; Jim Cole of Burnshall in Cudlipptown bought a Brough Superior, which was much admired. He had a box that slipped onto the sidecar attachment when working and he could change this for a proper seat if he wanted to give anyone a lift. Always on the lookout for a helping hand, Jim would tie his sheep dog to a bicycle to give him a pull if he felt tired. Others, like the Smales who lived opposite the inn and had a forge at Moorshop and only one pony, used the well-tried process of riding half a mile then leaving the pony to graze whilst another walked up to the pony and rode forward another half mile, doing turn and turn about.

Eliza Mudge of Sowtontown is off to market.

Horse, Jingle & Ralli Car

Johnnie Phillips of Youlditch used his ralli car to go shopping every Friday. He was the last farmer in the district to use a horse and trap and was regularly seen nodding off as the horse made its way home. Johnnie Phillips died in 1970 at the age of 84 years.

The horse omnibus making one of its last journeys to Lydford in 1930, with Bill Hawken in the driving seat.

For many centuries wheeled transport was unsuitable for the tracks and open space on the moor so sledges were used for moving loads which were too heavy for a packhorse. When it came to the cobbled or early metalled roads more sophisticated means became available and, perhaps surprisingly, many of these sprung vehicles seemed able to cope with even the rutted cart tracks to many farms. At Harford Bridge, Gerald Williamson has collected together a museum of these older vehicles and prepared a history of local horse transport.

Older villagers often refer to the 'jingle' as their childhood transport and that used by their parents well into the 1930s. This was more properly known as a 'governess' car and was brought into use around 1880. It had high sides and a rear entrance; the driver sat sideways to the horse so he could then keep an eye on the children. Older drivers, however, seem to have used a larger car such as the 'ralli' car, which was small, light and exceptionally strong. It was very much at home skipping through the fields and was in general use after 1910.

For those Victorians using the new railway to Tavistock South West Station, John Backwell of the Cornish Arms, West Street, Tavistock ran a horse omnibus service to Lydford on Monday and Friday and to Two Bridges on Tuesday, Wednesday and Friday. No doubt those from Peter Tavy without transport would have welcomed the lift to Harford Bridge before walking the rest of the way home. The service was finally withdrawn in 1930 as motor vehicles took over.

MEMORIES OF LIFE & LEISURE

Angela Larcombe

Life in Peter Tavy may seem as if it has continued in the same sleepy way for centuries, but of course the way of life of its people has changed just as it has elsewhere, only perhaps a little more slowly. Along with those who can recall walking miles to school in moorland snow and rarely going further than the local market, there are now other villagers who are connected with relatives and friends all over the world via the internet.

The village has had its share of dramas; a Victorian love triangle that ended in murder, a long-running court battle between moorland farmers, a notorious convict who patronised the local pub, and an appearance by Jimmy Savile, dressed in a gold lamé suit – certainly a first for the Peter Tavy Inn.

But these were events scattered through the years which were much discussed at the time, long remembered and passed on through generations. Life in the cottages and farms of the village was generally more humdrum and, certainly in the first half of the twentieth century, very hard work indeed.

Alec Phillott left school around the age of 14 to work as a gardener in Mary Tavy. He recalls that: 'My first job each morning was to go down to the well to collect two buckets of drinking water for the house.' When young Alec complained about his low wages of 15 shillings a week he was told he was being taught the value of money and that others were paid too much and did not appreciate it. Alec learnt his lesson and leaving the house, which was later sold to the Devonport Dockyard Orphanage, he went on to work with horses on a farm where, although he earned only 10 shillings a week, he had his board and lodging free.

Arthur Bellamy recollected the tough attitude of some Dartmoor farmers, accustomed as they were to wresting a hard living from the land. A man looking for work called at Collaton and George Mudge asked him if he had eaten. 'No, sir,' came the reply and the man was sent in for some breakfast before being told to fetch a horse from down the road. After some time the farmer went to see what was happening and saw the tackle hanging on the gate and the man with no idea of what to do. George said, 'No work, no food,' and kneed him in the stomach, making him vomit up his breakfast. The farmer then turned to his dog saying, 'You can have that, you do your work.'

In a more light-hearted memory Arthur tells how his uncle prepared the ground for the new Rectory and had to put in some explosives to clear rocks. He slung a set of chains over the rocks to hold them together but when he set the explosives off the chains were blown apart and he never saw them again.

Phyllis Dodd says that her father, Frederick William, was a Special Constable in the police force. Before war broke out they used to help guard places against the IRA. Once the group was guarding the railway bridge by the sugar factory at Half Bridge on the A386. The chap working with Frederick said, 'We must make sure we are on the Peter Tavy side if the bridge goes up!' Most of the time Frank Littlejohns of Harragrove partnered Phyllis' father.

Betty Wilton remembers the domestic arrangements at Standon. There was a cottage attached to the main house and in the room on the left there was a large water tank. Her mother had to go down and pump water up from the stream to fill it every morning, with separate water carried in a bucket for drinking. Alongside the water tank was a separator for the cream, which was put in a wide, round pan with a rope handle, and this she carried down to the stream to keep cool overnight. In the morning it was brought back to the kitchen where it was churned into butter and made into pats. The big house was connected to the kitchens on the ground floor through a door, which led directly into the dining room. Beyond the dining room was a hall with a beautiful wide staircase. The large sitting room had bay windows which looked out in two directions. Betty remembers that 'there was a bell pull which rang in the kitchen.' Later the house was altered, with part of the larger landing being made into a bathroom and the door leading to the second floor of the cottage being removed.

Radge Farm is an ancient house and is linked to the legend of Stephen's Grave – it was the scene of the attempted poisoning of Mary Bray. The occupant at the time of writing, May Wakeham, uses the old kitchen as a sitting room. In 1967 they blocked up the old fireplace, which had originally extended over the whole wall except for a recess near the window in which the cream for scalding was kept. They left the old grate and kept the old iron kettle with its tin lid, believed to have been the very one into which the

Below left: *Phyllis Dodd has lived in Chubb Farm all her life. She is the daughter of William Frederick and sister to William 'Bill' Dodd. A committed Methodist, her memories are to be found throughout this book.*

Below middle: *May Wakeham (née Medland) was born in Radge and has lived there all her life. Her parents had come to Radge in 1912. She recounts how, when they arrived at the farm, her parents had a 'suitcase of clothes and £9 in the pocket.' The Mary Dean Charity from whom she bought it shortly after her marriage in 1967 owned the farm on behalf of a school in Tamerton.*

Left: *Fred and Joan Amos came to live at Lucy Cottage in the 1960s when Fred retired. Joan worked at the inn and recounted tales of the Kray brothers and Frank Mitchell. It was at the inn that Fred met Robin Armstrong, the artist, and it is claimed that he encouraged Robin to give up his work as a water bailiff and concentrate on his paintings of wildlife. In his book* The Painted Stream, *Robin Armstrong recounts the conversation:*

Fred was looking at a picture of a wild
trout, lying on a table at the inn,
'Ad few o' they in moi time.' More than
a few, I thought – and a salmon or two
as well no doubt.
'Some big 'uns too,' he said, reading my
thoughts with a gap-tooth grin.
'Course it was all a long time ago…yer, a long
time ago,' he sighed.
Fred straightened up. 'You'm a fair bit of a
drawrer, Robbie,' he said and took a long
swig of mild. I moved swiftly forward and
hastily moved the watercolour out of
danger. I needn't have worried. Wiping
his grizzled beard with the back of his hand,
Fred said, 'Why don't 'ee write a book?'

Right: *Alec Phillott was born in Somerset but his mother came from Cudlipptown and was the daughter of William Arthur, who farmed at Kinsmans before taking on Higher Creason in Horndon. Alec came to farm at Brousentor in 1954 where he lost most of his sheep to a disease called braxi in his first year. He recovered partly due to taking a job as a MoD range warden.*

Above: *Peggy Stephens (née Land) was born at Willsworthy and has moved around the parish. They were the last to live at Kinsmans. In 1951 she was at Longbettor, and again her family were the last to live there. In 1958 she married Douglas Stephens and came to live in the village. Known to everyone in the village, like her mother before her, she is always ready to help everyone.*

spurned lover dropped the poison. 'Even as late as 1966 the floor in here was compacted earth.' Outside the house is a small annexe where the servants used to sleep, probably including Mary Bray when she came down from Godsworthy. Its rough stone walls are clearly much older than the outer wall of the present house.

Life may have been hard but most country families benefited from good, fresh food and many older villagers remember making butter and cream. Jessie Cole used to take her butter and cream to market at Tavistock. Moorview, at Cudlipptown, has a cellar with a lined salting box for keeping meat through the winter.

Peggy Stephens remembers that when her mother was a housekeeper at Kinsmans she used to help Mr Reep at Gnattor by churning the butter and skimming the cream. Peggy's family was the last to live at Kinsmans, which is now in ruins. She remembers hurting her leg badly one day when helping Mrs Rowse with a calf: 'I started screaming because the blood was running down my leg.' Mrs Sarah Cole, who lived with her husband Walter in the nearby cottage, had been a nurse and she singed a piece of torn sheet in front of the fire and wrapped up Peggy's leg. The doctor sent young Peggy to hospital to have it stitched, but when they made her stay overnight in the women's ward she was frightened. When her mother visited her the next day she refused to stay any longer.

With Princetown only a few miles away across the moor it is not surprising that escaped prisoners sometimes made their way to the village. In 1939, when Peggy Stephens' family lived at Longbettor, two convicts escaped from Dartmoor Prison. She recalls that, 'Late that afternoon a man appeared at Gnattor where mother worked. It was clear he was one of the convicts and he looked exhausted.' Her mother took him in and asked about the other man. He was outside, too afraid to come in. They had both swum the Tavy and were cold and wet. She took them in and gave them the rabbit pie she had in the oven for Mr Reep. When they had finished and rested she called the police. The next day she and Mr Reep appeared in the papers and were thanked by the authorities and the prisoners.

Not all escaped prisoners were likely to be met with a welcome. The notorious Frank Mitchell, rumoured to have links with the Krays, is said to have regularly drunk at the Peter Tavy Inn while on a working party and it was strongly rumoured the Krays organised his escape in the mid 1960s. Joan Amos recalls her husband Fred sleeping with a shotgun handy while 'Axeman' Mitchell was on the run. Gordon Gregory, a village man who gave evidence at the trial of the Kray brothers, later met with a mysterious death. He was found lying in the road near Churchtown. The inquest concluded that he had run into a group of ponies in the mist and was

SHE MADE CONVICTS A DINNER

WHILE 100 warders, soldiers and 200 police, drenched to the skin, were searching Dartmoor yesterday in blinding rain for two escaped convicts, their quarry were seated before a roaring farmhouse fire, tucking into rabbit pie and chatting gaily to a thirty-six-year-old woman to whom they had surrendered.

Before they sat down to dine the men asked that the prison governor should be informed where they were, and then they gratefully changed into dry clothing.

The two runaways, Reginald Mead, thirty-one, and Albert Alfred Beard, thirty-eight, had been on the run for nearly ten hours in a heavy storm.

They broke out of Dartmoor Prison just before dawn, sawing away the iron bars of their cells with hacksaws which they had managed to smuggle out of the prison tool shop.

Hiding behind rocks when in danger of being seen, they headed for Tavistock.

Soon after their escape they were creeping along a river bank when they fell into one of the dreaded Dartmoor bogs. Both managed to cling to the banks and pull themselves out, but they lost their boots.

Tired and exhausted, they made their way to an isolated farmhouse eight miles from the gaol. They knocked at the door, told the woman who opened it who they were, and asked for a cup of tea

She Wasn't Frightened

The woman, Mrs Amelia Lamb, housekeeper at Nattor Farm, Peter Tavy, asked them inside.

Mrs Lamb told the *Daily Mirror*: "They looked absolutely done in They were wet through

While they warmed themselves in front of the fire I found them some dry clothes and got them a meal ready

They then sat down to the table and had some rabbit pie and a cake I had just made.

I was not at all frightened. When you live so far from anywhere you don't get that way."

Mr John Reep, the farmer, was at the back of the house when the convicts called.

He told the *Daily Mirror*:

"They seemed really decent chaps. They were very well behaved.

"When they left they thanked my housekeeper and myself for what we had done for them

They did not talk very much about their escape. They said they had no complaints about their treatment in the prison, but it was just a case of doing anything to get liberty.

They said they wished they had not done it as they had only harmed themselves."

SOVIE BOM

RUSSIAN w machine and children li other towns in

Finns clear bomber, shot twenty people amazed to th woman.

She was one o who took part in More raids are for the week-enc desire to allow from Helsinki

Heavy Rus

Official figu people have b in raids.

Russian troops they are trying t

A cutting from the Daily Mirror *from Monday 4 December 1939 recounts the escape of two prisoners from Dartmoor Prison who were befriended by Peggy Stephens' mother, Mrs Land, not Lamb as stated.*

Above: The 'new' Rectory was built in 1911/12. It has a separate entrance to the right of the front door, giving entry to the rector's study. Sunday school children and official visitors used this door. After the First World War the gardens were laid out and a tennis court laid for the use of parishioners. The house was sold by the Church authorities in 1966 and has been appropriately renamed Glebe House.

Opposite below: The 'old' Rectory shown here is not the earliest. There is no clear record as to the where-abouts of the original building referred to in 1680 as a 'little house, with kitchen and chamber over, a porch and dairy'. It may well have been on the site of the one in the photo which, built by the Revd John Gilbert in 1724, was clearly a bigger house and the Terrier describes it as being divided into inner and outer houses. The house was of stone and the inner house had a slated roof, with the outer house thatched. The former comprised a parlour with boarded floor, a kitchen with a stone-flagged floor with four chambers over and a hall with an earth floor. The latter contained a brewhouse, dairy and cellar with four chambers over. In addition there was a barn and a stable – also two small gardens, two orchards, a bowling alley, two courts and a mowplot. This picture, taken c.1900, shows Mrs Bryant with her son and daughter.

kicked to death when he came off his motorcycle. But it is claimed in the village that his bike was standing up against the hedge and the bruising he had sustained was only on his head and the upper part of his body. Was he murdered by one of the Kray gang?

There is a lifetime of memories in the village. Even those who have lived here for just 20 or 30 years have seen many changes. The school, shop and Post Office have gone and Peter Tavy no longer has its own 'homegrown' milk, which used to be bottled and delivered by the Dodds. But there is a new live-ly base at the Village Hall where one can play whist, learn to weave, attend a concert, or enjoy one of the many workshops which are held to teach everything from various crafts to circus skills. Peter Tavy retains its community spirit as it goes into the twenty-first century.

Water Supply

The supply of water for drinking seems not to have troubled the villagers of Peter Tavy until well into the last century. Elsie Jeffery recalled that during her childhood, early in the century, a man would come from the rectory twice a day to fill his buckets at the village well behind the house called Midhurst. Mrs Weeks at the shop is recorded as saying she had drunk the water from the well all her life, as had most of the village, and come to no harm. There were other wells at the Inn, Higher Churchtown and Higher Mill, and in some of the outlying farms water is still obtained from such wells, although others draw their water from the streams and local springs. In 1909 some concern had been expressed about water supplies for the expanding village, especially during the summer, and Tavistock Rural Council, whose responsibility it was at the time, approached the Roskilly family about constructing a reservoir in Mill Meadow. The Roskillys responded with the gift of sufficient land for the reservoir and Revd Kempe, the landlord of Higher Mill, agreed to the reservoir, 'as long as W. Williams (the miller) has all the water he needs.' A concrete-enclosed reservoir was built and connected to a circuit of standpipes to serve the village. Taps were placed at Southditch, Coombe Cottages, Lower Churchtown, the Reading Room, close to the Village Bridge and at the side of Chubb Farm. The small reservoir at Mill Meadow proved inadequate and a second reservoir was built on the north bank of Colley Brook above the Coombe Clam. A few houses on the northern side of the village seem to have had piped water into the house, but this was very rare and it was not until 1967 that additional work was undertaken to connect everybody in the village to a mains water supply. Even this took time and in 1968 a Mrs Pinhey complained that 'if you fill a glass with water from the tap there is quarter of an inch of sediment in it.' She added that she never drank the water and depended on bottled lemonade and sherry!

Water not used for drinking, known as slops by the village, can still be seen running in an open stream from the Causeway, passing the Village Hall, where it goes into a pipe to cross under the road and reappears outside Wisdom, down Village Way to run into the fields at Churchtown, where the cattle enjoy it. Phyllis Dodd recalls how there was a small 'waterfall' outside the Village Hall at one time, from which water could be drawn easily with a bucket. During renova-tion, when the stream's bed was cobbled, this facility was lost. There is still no sewerage in the village and most houses have septic tanks or soakaway systems.

One of the village standpipes outside Coombe Cottages.

'Polly' Abel at the pump drawing water from the well at Lower Godsworthy.

The First World War

Arthur Bellamy of Wedlake, brother to Francis Bellamy and Jessie Cole, was born in 1895. Like many young men he signed up in 1914 at the very start of the war. His verses, shown overleaf, were sent to his parents with letters home and describe his feelings, and no doubt those of many others, during those four years. Serving with the Royal Devon Yeomanry, he died on the Somme on 2 September 1918.

Six men from Peter Tavy lost their lives in the First World War. As well as Arthur Bellamy, Arthur Worth, George Edward Mudge, Fred Rice, George Maddock and Richard Reddicliffe died whilst serving their country. During the preparation of this book Richard Reddicliffe's medals and the Bronze Death Plaque were found.

For those at home in Peter Tavy, the First World War had knock-on effects, particularly for the farmers. James Perkins remembered helping his father drive very small ponies to Tavistock market, where they sold for up to £100 each for work in the pits. The ponies had a 'mealy' nose (light brown) and were very small – true Dartmoor ponies. They were quite scarce and it was difficult to find the right ones for the pits. Similarly, during those years cows were sold for up to £100 each – there were good prices at Goose Fair, especially if you could get a cow to calve about ten days before the fair, but prices fell again swiftly at the end of hostilities.

The Death Plaque of Richard Reddicliffe, Corporal in the Royal Devon Hussars. Death plaques similar to this one were made from solid bronze and sent to the families of all soldiers who died in the First World War.

In the year 1914,
The time of the Worldwide War,
Our regiment of yeomen were ordered
To camp on the Essex shore.

We were there to repulse an invasion
By Germany over the sea.
We were there until trained and ready
In the foremost of battles to be.

We were lusty and proud of our manhood
As we trailed and scouted like men
Hard hit and reliant
By the use of the gun and the spade.

We trenched, manoeuvred and battled
In many a mimic affray,
Each man looked forward with eagerness
To the call that was coming someday.

But in time we grew lighthearted
And so did our officers too
For weeks slipped into months as we waited
For the Germans over the blue.

We galloped like madness o'er the country
Playing with rifle and blank,
We signalled and scouted and filed
And every kind of prank.

We thrust into haystacks with bayonets
We cut turnips in half with our sword
But still from the War Office in London
There came not a single word.

At last from o'er seas came a pleading
Of our heroes in distress
Our regiment to help them were drafted
Away from our east coast rest.

It was a quiet autumn eve
The last week of September
We sailed away from Liverpool
The farewell all remember.

It was on a White Star liner
The Olympic was her name.
We left our home for overseas
Hoping all would play the game.

We sailed along the Irish sea
And through the Biscay Bay
And reached the mighty fortress Gib.
Late on the following day.

Whilst steaming through the Med.
Exciting was the scene,
As a torpedo launched at our ship
From a German submarine
(12 feet too close, 1,200 on board).

A French crew numbering 33
We picked up on that day.
The pirates had sunk their transport ship
And they had lost their way.

The sun had set beyond the hills
And the stars shone bright and gay
When the laden ship Osmaria
Left the base at Midress Bay.

We sailed along the Adrian Sea
'til Salva was in sight
As soon as we saw our battleships
Pumping leadite left and right.

We anchored in the Bay that night
For seas were rough and wild,
But on the next day on the beach
And up the ravine we filed.

The following were our evening hymns
When the nights were bright and fine
Sung by many a Devonshire lad
In those solitary front lines.

Sing me to sleep where the bullets fall,
Let me forget the war and all
Damp is my dugout, cold my feet,
Biscuits and bully all to eat.

Sing me to sleep where the bombs explode,
And shrapnel shell on our abode.
Over the sandbags helmets you'll find
Graves in front and graves behind.

Sing me to sleep in some old shed
As dangers rattle around my head
Stretched out on my waterproof
Dodging the raindrops thro' the roof.

Sing me to sleep and let me wake
To find all wars have been ceased…

Arthur Bellamy. Corporal in the Royal Devon
Yeomanry, lost his life in September 1918.

*The 'Con Nuts' from Tavistock, 'A' Company 5th Devons.
Alfred Leetoose is second from the right but others said to
come from Peter Tavy have not been identified. This postcard
was sent in 1914 from the Punjab. Alf writes that 'this area
is known for its dust graveyards and beggars, how different
from Peter Tavy!'*

*The Peter Tavy War Memorial was erected and dedicated in
1922. It was paid for entirely by the subscriptions of people
living in the parish. Remembrance services have been held
around the memorial on the Sunday nearest to 11 November
annually ever since. The names of those who lost their lives
in the Second World War were inscribed in 1948.*

The Second World War

It might have been expected that the parish would be insulated from many of the troubles of the Second World War, and indeed it was. That is not to say that the conflict had no impact. Perhaps one of the earliest changes was the formation of the Home Guard.

Under the experienced eye of John Vogwill and John Roskilly some 30 volunteers were recruited to the Local Defence Volunteers (LDV) at the beginning of the Second World War. Although they had no uniforms, the group began training at once with marches out to Cudlipptown and back through Horndon and the main road to Harford Bridge. During the bitter evenings of 1939–40 they received talks from Army officers in the schoolroom. The uniforms arrived and were stored at Lang Cottage (now Spring House) under the eye of Herbert Stevens, who was also responsible for ammunition; the change of name to the Home Guard came soon after this. At first the only guns carried were their own shotguns with ball cartridges, but later they were issued with Army .303 rifles. Their duties included guarding the power station at Mary Tavy overnight and the bridges at Harford Bridge, as well as look-out posts on Cox Tor and Smear Ridge.

Consisting of farmers, quarrymen, teachers and bank clerks – some over the maximum age for call-up to the Armed Forces, others in reserved occupations – they took their duties seriously but with good humour. James Perkins recalled how he would ride up on horseback with Dennis Cannon every morning, before starting work on the farm, to do two hours' 'look-out' at Cox Tor. Phyllis Dodd remembers how

Home Guard, 1943. Left to right, back row: *F.J. Roskilly (Nutley), W. Smale (village blacksmith),*
J. Perkins (Gatehouse), T. Medland (Radge), J. Cole (Burnshall, Cudlipptown), F. Collins (Higher Mill);
middle row: *E. Pellowe, J. Osborne, G. Medland, A. Perkins (Tortown), E. Pengelly, J. Mudge (Sowtontown),*
Mr Simms (bank manager in Plymouth), J. Blowey, B. Rickard (bus driver, Shula); front row: *J. Bellamy,*
Mr Wedd (headmaster, Mount House School), F. Alford (Cudlipptown), S.D. Stratford, J. Vogwill (Moor View),
J.M. Roskilly senr (Nutley), Henry H. Stevens (Lang Cottage), F. Brooks, G. Mudge (Sowtontown).

her father, Frederick William, did guard duty at Harford Bridge with Frank Littlejohn. They used to joke about which side of the bridge they might be on if they were blown up and whether they would be able to get back to the village if the Tavy was in flood! Once a month, usually on a Sunday, they would go out to the Butts at Willsworthy for rifle practice. Some were not as accurate as might have been expected, considering that they owned shotguns. The Army sergeant inspecting the rifles before firing was known for his views of the Home Guard and his descriptive vocabulary!

With their Army experience John Vogwill and John Roskilly kept up the pressure on training and exercises. Sometimes it was a mock invasion, on other occasions a local disaster with many wounded. On one such event Eddie Pellowe and John Palmer, neither being very tall, had the job of carrying John Roskilly on a stretcher as a casualty from Cudlipptown to the rectory in Peter Tavy, which was the designated headquarters and first-aid post, a Devon mile by any standard! It was hard labour after a day's work but as James Perkins once said, with his characteristic wry smile, 'It must have worked as we were not invaded.'

A searchlight crew was stationed above Wedlake and on Whit Tor, and the muddy lanes had to be made up with stone and gravel to carry the lorries.

At first this was done, both here and at Baggator, by convicts from Dartmoor Prison, but at a later stage German prisoners of war and even the American Army were used! The moor itself was used extensively for training and Standon was soon taken over as a base for the Marines. Many years later it was the Marines, during a change-over weekend, that finally set the house on fire in an attempt to relight some smouldering peat with petrol. It was too remote for fire engines to reach and all but the wing of the house burnt down.

A unit of the Royal Electical and Mechanical Engineers was stationed at Pitts Cleave, where they built the Nissen huts and established a practice firing range, and a large camp was set up on Cox Tor for American troops before the Normandy invasion.

Two planes crashed on Standon Down; one British and one German. The British plane was a bomber with his load still up, but the pilot managed to land it and with great care the bombs were successfully removed. Several villagers remember how the plane had to be dismantled after attempts to take a 'Queen Mary' truck up the Cudlipptown road failed dismally, with it completely blocking the road. The lorries were then parked in Church Lane, whilst the airmen lodged in the village at Wisdom and Higher Mill, and the plane was brought down piecemeal.

Special Police, 1942. Left to right, back row: Bert Bellamy, William F. Dodd (Chubb Farm), Stan Cole (Mary Tavy), Harold Bellamy, Bill Bellamy (Churchtown), Frank Littlejohn (Harragrove); front row: Arthur Sleeman (Homefield), Sgt George Giles (Harford House), P.C. Anstey (Mary Tavy & Peter Tavy Police), Bert Bellamy (Edgcombe), Thomas Vogwill (Shula).

DEVON COUNTY
WAR AGRICULTURAL EXECUTIVE COMMITTEE.

DEFENCE REGULATIONS, 1939.
THE CULTIVATION OF LANDS ORDER, 1939.

To ......F. W. Collins, Esq.,..

of .... Higher Mills,..

.... Peter Tavy, Tavistock.

in the County of Devon or other the occupier of the land described in the Schedule hereto.

THE DEVON WAR AGRICULTURAL EXECUTIVE COMMITTEE, being the body authorised to exercise on behalf of the Minister of Agriculture and Fisheries within the Administrative County of Devon the powers in that behalf conferred by Regulation 62 (1) of the Defence Regulations, 1939, hereby direct you to carry out in respect of the land described in the Schedule hereto the works of cultivation specified in the said Schedule.

Failure to comply with this direction or any part thereof is an offence under the Defence Regulations.

Dated ......26.8.42.......................... ... ...19........

By Order of the Executive Committee.
Signed

BRADNINCH HALL,
        CASTLE STREET, EXETER.

Telephone : Exeter 54991/54992.

Chairman of the Executive Committee.

SCHEDULE.

P.E. 51475

District	Parish	Ordnance Map No. and Edition.	Area	Description	Required Cultivation
			Acres		
Area 13.	Peter Tavy.	503	1.954	Arable.	To cultivate & till to DREDE CORN for harvest in 1943, manage & harvest in a husbandlike manner.
	Pt.	504	.750	"	To cultivate & till to POTATOES for harvest in 1943, manage & harvest in a husbandlike manner
	Pt.	504	.889	"	To cultivate & till to GREEN CROP for harvest in 1943, manage & harvest in a husbandlike manner.

This order is also hereby served on your landlord:-

Messrs. Chilatt & Pearse, Solicitors,

A copy of a wartime agriculture order in 1942, which required Frank Collins 'to grow, harvest and manage in a husbandlike manner dredge corn, potatoes, and a green crop,' in his fields at Coombeparks, during the 1943 season.

A class of local ladies at Whitchurch on a course on dairy work, 1945.

A German plane came down during a raid on Plymouth; two of the crew walked down to Baggator and gave themselves up to Miss Pereira and Miss Chapman who lived there. George Giles, a police sergeant of the Special Police who lived in Harford House, came up when he saw the plane crash and took the German airmen into custody.

A British Spitfire came down on Whit Tor towards the end of the war. Richard Friend was working in a field near Hillbridge and saw the plane come in from the moor very low, following the line of the Tavy. It then turned, coming back up to the moor, travelling very fast. Dick turned to the man he was working with and said, 'It will never turn without hitting the tor.' Almost at once they heard the crash. They rushed off up the lane but by the time they reached the tor they could see the blaze and the pilot had not escaped.

During the war every farmer had to devote some of his land to corn, oats or barley. Even on farms in the outlying areas such as Baggator, farmers like Jack Palmer ploughed for oats, but generally potatoes or mangolds were more common away from the village. Frederick Dodd and his neighbour Frank Collins both grew potatoes in the south-facing fields of the Coombe. These were stored in clamps under the hedges, covered with corrugated iron and hedge clippings or fern, until they were wanted. Frank Collins, occasionally venturing into growing corn, had the help of George Abel when it came to threshing, for he himself was growing oats at Twist (Twyste).

Almost everyone with a corner of land kept a pig. Peggy Stephens recalls that when they were first sent for slaughter, the pigs were graded and the family were allowed to keep half a pig for themselves, so long as they forfeited 26 weeks' of bacon ration.

Another tale tells of how a pig fattened illegally by a farmer was killed and cut up to be brought to the owner after dark. The children were sent to bed early that night. The pig was then rapidly salted and stored in earthenware pots for later use. The backyard where all this was done would have been carefully washed and swept down to erase footprints and tyre tracks. The narrator of this memory said 'I was told that I must never mention what had happened to anyone, else they would all go to prison. It was many years before I mentioned it to a soul.'

Whilst the men were busy with the Home Guard and Special Police, many of the ladies joined the Women's Voluntary Services (WVS), now the WRVS. Mrs Cross, wife of Commander Geoffrey Cross of the Hermitage, led them by holding afternoon and evening meetings at her house, at which they would knit scarves, gloves or mittens. In hard winters the younger ladies would go to the houses of the older villagers to make sure they were all right.

Jessie Bellamy recalled German prisoners of war working on the farms before the war had ended. It was forbidden to pay them, so her husband gave each man who had worked on the farm a suit before he left to return to Germany at the end of the war.

Final victory was not celebrated until VJ Day, Victory over Japan. A bonfire was lit on Cox Tor to celebrate, but one boy threw a closed bottle of paraffin onto the fire and then shouted for everyone to run away. It exploded, showering the area with burning sticks!

In Memoriam

Four men from Peter Tavy lost their lives in the Second World War: John G.W. Doidge, Thomas Roskilly, George W. Wren and Arthur Thomas.

High Days & Holidays

Donna Baker

Peter Tavy has always known how to enjoy itself. From coronations to jubilees, from garden parties to village fêtes – no excuse for a party has ever been missed. Nor have the celebrations been ordinary or 'run-of-the-mill'. The tradition for having something 'different' seems to have begun well before living memory and is still going strong today, as was proved at the 2001 Village Fayre, when 40 teddy bears bungee-jumped bravely from the church tower and several hundred yellow plastic ducklings raced pell-mell down the Colley Brook.

Let's look at some of the earliest recollections. An annual fête or fair seems to have been a must, bringing folk from all the surrounding hamlets and villages, as well as from Peter Tavy itself. At one time the yearly event was held in the garden of the Lodge, now know as the Hermitage, although latterly it has moved to the more central location of the

Village Hall and Methodist church. There in the Lodge grounds the schoolteacher Mrs Sleeman, a 'very quaint and old-fashioned lady', would tell fortunes from cards. She may have foretold many fortunes but did she also foretell her own or, meticulous to the penny with her money, did she not need the cards to know that she would die worth 'quite a few thousand' pounds?

Guessing the weight of the sheep is another tradition that remains today. Eileen Duncan is proud of having won the competition twice and then gone on to another fair to do the same again. In 1997 it was won by an Australian visitor who wasn't a sheep farmer – just a good guesser. That same year a set of stocks was erected for village folk to throw wet sponges at the bellringers; either the sponges weren't wet enough or the villagers' hearts weren't in it, for the ringers still practise assiduously every week.

CONCERT

AT ST. PETER TAVY,

In aid of the Football Club,

SATURDAY, JANUARY 27th, 1900.

PROGRAMME.

Part 1.

1 PIANO SOLO ... ... MISS EMMA HOLMES
2 FOOTBALL SONG AND CHORUS } "Our Football Team" THE FOOTBALL CLUB.
3 SONG ... ... "Roses underneath the Snow" MISS M. MILMAN.
4 SONG ... ... "The Turnit Hoer" ... ... MR. HORNE.
5 VOCAL DUET "Music sweet shall flow To-night" { MISS VOGWILL and MR. T. ASH.
6 SONG ... ... "A May Morning" ... MISS ARGALL.
7 SONG ... ... "You've got a long way to go" MR. T. HOLMES.
8 SONG ... ... "Only the Dickybirds know" ... MISS ROWE.
   Comic Song "Too Big" Mr F Williams
9 VOCAL DUET "Sally, Sally, Sially, Shally" { MISS MILMAN and MR. G. EDWARDES.
10 SONG ... ... "Soldier's Tear" ... MISS ABRAHALL.
11 Comic Song ... ... "Too Big" ... Mr. F. WILLIAMS.
12 RECITATION ... ... MR. P. BRYANT.
13 COMIC SONG ... "All that I could Spare" ...MR. W. STEVENS.

Part 2.

1 FOOTBALL SONG AND CHORUS "Kick Boys, Kick" FOOTBALL CLUB.
2 VOCAL DUET "Whisper, and I shall hear" { MISS MILMAN and MR. G. EDWARDES.
3 SONG ... ... "Willie, we have missed you" MISS VOGWILL.
4 SONG ... "The Charge of the 21st Lancers" ... MR. T. ASH.
5 SONG ... ... "Beauty's Eyes" ... MISS ARGALL.
6 SONG ... ... "It's easy if you try" MR. JOHN VOGWILL.
7 DUET "Country Courtship" { MISS ROWE and MR. ALFRED BRIMMACOMBE.
8 COMIC SONG ... "The Evening News" ... MR. W. STEVENS.
9 SONG ... ... MISS F. BRYANT.
10 SONG ... ... MR. HORNE.
11 SONG ... ... "Soldiers in the Park" MISS ABRAHALL.
12 SONG ... ... "Soldiers of the Queen" ... MR. GIDLEY.

GOD SAVE THE QUEEN.

THE TAVISTOCK PRINTING COMPANY, LIMITED.

Peter Tavy Annual Sports.

President - Rev. Austin Lester.

Programme of Concert.

Part 1.

1 Pianoforte Solo ... ... MRS. WREN
2 Song, "The Carnival" ... MISS TAPSON
3 Comic Song (Selected) MR. R. WEATHERBY
4 Song ... ... REV. AUSTIN LESTER
5 Violin Solo (Selected) ... ... MR. CUDDEFORD
6 Duet, "Weary Willie and Tired Tim" MESSRS. WILLIAMS & PHILLIPS
7 Song, "Mona" ... ... MR. T. ASH
8 Comic Song, "I'll be cross, Arabella, I'll be cross" MR. A. DOUCH
9 Song, "I want my Mammy, yes, I do" MISS OLIVE ROGERS
10 Song... ... ... MR. C. PILLAR
11 Comic Song ... ...MR. WEATHERBY

Part 2.

12 Pianoforte Solo ... ... MISS HOLMES
13 Song... ... ... REV. AUSTIN LESTER
14 Comic Song, "John Willie, come on" MR. A. DOUCH
15 Violin Solo ... ... MR. CUDDEFORD
16 Duet, "Sweet Nightingale" MISS MILLMAN AND MR. ASH
17 Song, "Shadowland" ... ... MISS TAPSON
18 Song, "Stay in your own backyard" MISS OLIVE ROGERS
19 Song, "The Gates of Paradise" MR. T. H. ASH
20 Miniature Minstrels MESSRS. DOUCH, WILLIAMS, WEATHERBY AND PHILLIPS
21 Song, "There's a Land" ... ... MISS MILMAN

GOD SAVE THE KING.

H. Pillar & Son, Printers, Tavistock.

Concert programme in aid of the Football Club, 1900.
Thomas Ash was particularly appreciated
for his fine voice.

Concert programme in aid of the Annual Sports,
during the First World War.

Taken in 1923, this picture of the 'bonnet competition' seems to show much greater enthusiasm from the men than the ladies. Perhaps the ladies were exhausted after making the hats for the men!

The Lamerton Hunt meets outside Gatehouse in 1911. The West Dartmoor and Spooners Hunt also came regularly to the moors above the village.

Tug o' War with James Perkins in charge. A regular favourite among the young men of the village.

The earliest report we have of a royal celebration comes from the *Tavistock Gazette* of 1897, when Queen Victoria's Golden Jubilee was commemorated 'from morn till dewy eve', beginning with a service in the church and going on to a substantial dinner in the schoolroom, which was tastefully decorated with national flags, with 'all distinctions removed', and everyone from General Elderton, the local hero of the Indian Mutiny, to the humblest parishioner sitting at the same table and 'drinking from the same cup'. Scarcely had the dinner gone down than the gathering moved to a field 'kindly lent by Messrs W.J. Dodd and E.G. Bray' for an afternoon of sports, including a strenuous tug-of-war, and when that was over it was back to the schoolroom for tea – also substantial! Then off everyone went again to the sports field to finish the games and award the prizes and, as if that was not enough, a bonfire was lit on Smeardon at 10p.m. and fireworks lit the sky. The bells, which had been provided with new frames and ropes from the Jubilee Fund, were rung at intervals from beginning to end. The parish must have rung too, with shouts and cheers all day long.

It is Empire Day that is recorded in the photograph showing a large party of children, all dressed up in their Sunday best, beneath a banner proclaiming: 'God for the Children: The future Builders of This Mighty Empire' *(see page 6)*. Those children have now passed on; some of them have fought in

one or both of the two world wars of the twentieth century, but many of them probably bore the names still familiar today – Abel, Dodd, Stephens, Bellamy, Mudge and so on – and many of their descendants must still be in the village.

Subsequent royal occasions were celebrated with similar events and the decorated cups, saucers and mugs that still take pride of place today on many a kitchen dresser. In 1953, for Queen Elizabeth II's Coronation, the BBC broadcast a service from the church, with a warning on the programme against 'shuffling or knocking of feet and jingling of money in pockets', and the villagers were all told to look out for Revd Pratt wiping his nose at the end of the last hymn, this being the sign for an extra verse to be sung. However, many found themselves confused at the end of this hymn, unable to remember whether it meant they were or were not to sing another verse!

The Queen's Silver Jubilee was celebrated in 1977 with a similar programme, including a number of sports for children – running races, egg-and-spoon races, wheelbarrow and three-legged races – and more bell-ringing and 'substantial' teas before the beacon was lit on Smeardon and another fireworks display held. It was at one of these displays that someone forgot to close the lid of the wooden trunk that the fireworks were kept in, with what could have been disastrous results when a spark set light to everything in it. Fortunately, nobody was hurt and the display that night was extra spectacular, but soon over.

A different kind of occasion was the regular meet of the Lamerton hunt outside the double doors of Gatehouse Barn. With the church tower in the

Gillian Miles, a television personality, opens the Village Fête with Ken Ball, 1982.

Bobbie Cox, an international weaver and designer, shows young Shaun McCance the secrets of spinning.

Penelope Baker and Mark Meadowcroft take two young ladies for a donkey ride.

background, the village would turn out to watch the gentlemen of the hunt in their pink coats and help pass round the stirrup-cup. This is one colourful but controversial tradition that looks like coming to an end in the early years of the twenty-first century.

In 1987, Peter Tavy hit the national headlines with quite a different event – the Great Television Switch-Off. The *Daily Mirror* picked the village to participate in an experiment with a week of television deprivation, just to see if life could be lived without such necessities as *Coronation Street* and *Crossroads*. For some, it wasn't a problem – Bill Dodd was photographed by a newspaper cheerfully using his TV set as a milking stool, although he did add that he wouldn't have been so ready to switch it off had it meant missing *One Man and His Dog*. Other experimenters, however, fell by the wayside; one to watch a documentary on the *Lost Cities of the Incas* and another who tuned in for both *Coronation Street* and *This is Your Life*.

It seems to have been a relief to everyone when Jimmy Savile himself, resplendent in gold lamé trousers, arrived on the Sunday to declare the village switched on again. Perhaps the programmes really were better then. Surrounded by children waving 'Jim'll Switch It' banners, he spent the afternoon in the Village Hall, where he signed autographs, chatted and raffled what else but a colour television set and video recorder, donated by the *Daily Mirror*, along with a cheque for £1,000 towards a new roof for the Village Hall. Peter Tavy's fame had spread far and after this event Ann and Chris Pollard, who ran the shop and Post Office, were inundated all week with telephone calls from radio stations all over the world. But even then it wasn't all over, for each family was visited by researchers wanting to know just how they had managed without the 'one-eyed monster' in the corner. 'A lot of DIY', local newspaper reporter Angela Larcombe commented, 'and quite a lot of swearing as well'. On the Monday evening, when the dust had settled and the cameras disappeared, there was just one more thing to do – go along to the Village Hall to see the video recordings of all the soaps they'd missed!

The Sports Day was an annual event for many years and programmes dated around 1900 show that a concert was a vital part of the proceedings. We can imagine the villagers settling back to listen to the pianoforte solos performed by Miss Holmes, the duets of Miss Milman and Mr Edwards, the comic songs *John Willie, come on* and *I'll be cross, Arabella, I'll be cross*, sung by Mr A. Douch and, since this particular concert was in aid of the Football Club, what surely must have been the highlight of the evening: *Our Football Team*, sung by the entire club.

Football leapt into prominence again in 1944 when, despite the war, Peter Tavy managed to muster a team to challenge the Royal Marines and beat them 3-2. Led by Revd Pratt and the 'man of the match' – a 48-year-old known as 'Kerlo' – the local side drew on a number of skills barred to present-day footballers, such as 'bumping, pushing, charging, jumping, acrobatic somersaults, air leaps and ground sprawls', and the shouts of encouragement could 'almost be heard at the other end of Dartmoor'. Scornful comparisons were made in the local press with the £100,000 forward line of Blackpool and one exhausted marine was carried off on a stretcher to the tune *Old Soldiers Never Die* played on a cornet. Afterwards, to rub salt into the wounds, the 'Royals' entertained the 'Coombes' to a 'delicious spread'. Let it never be said that Peter Tavy passes up the chance of a good meal.

Through it all, the village fêtes and fairs continued as the backbone of village entertainment, always with that 'something different'. A photograph of a 'bonnet competition' shows men and women of the village suitably arrayed – the men's bonnets being very much more elaborate than the women's. Another picture shows several hay-bales and a row of rubber tyres set up as an obstacle course and of course there were always plenty of stalls and sideshows: throwing the horseshoe, riding the slippery pole, skittles, darts, bowling, strawberries and cream, junket and cream, hat-trimming, penny on a plate, coconut shies, toys, books, produce, needlework exhibitions, fortune telling, balloons, pony rides and, on occasion, 'a game of chance featuring a tame white mouse with the brightest pink eyes imaginable'. Quite what the game was seems to have been forgotten, although perhaps not by the mouse!

Once again, in the mid 1960s, money raised was to go towards a new roof for the Village Hall – something that seems to have occurred roughly every 20 years. It's all part of the tradition. And the traditions go on. Small things may change: the slippery pole gives way to the duck race, the men's bonnet competition to the teddy-bear bungee-jump, and some, like the hunt, may come to an end. Yet the greatest tradition of all goes on – that of village life, a procession of fêtes and fairs, sports days and village quizzes, entertainments and games; a continuing celebration of events great and small, binding together the inhabitants of one small cluster of homes to form a real, living community. This tradition is alive and well in the village of Peter Tavy.

The assembled group in Old Sports Field, below the Reading Room in 1932. Left to right:
T. Driver, G. Rooke, G. Mudge, J. Thomas, J. Perkins, B. Sellick, G. Lane, K. Sellick, A. Sleeman,
J. Phillips, J. Bellamy, L. Ash, F. Collins, B. Sellick, A. Rooke, W. Bellamy senr, M. Holmes,
Cdr Cross, J. Lane, Revd Pratt, J. Vogwill, Mrs Vogwill, P. Thomas, Mrs Sleeman, B. Taylor,
J. Mudge, Mrs Rooke, J. Bellamy, W. Lennard, J. Bray, C. Stratford.

Following the Walkham when 'Beating the Bounds', 2000. Too much enthusiasm at the front,
but everyone got round the 28 miles done on the second day!

Beating the Bounds

The tradition of beating the bounds goes back to Saxon times when the people of a settlement were organised into manors and needed to be shown the extent or boundaries of the lord of the manor's land. The word 'bound' refers to a stone or boundary marker that was struck with a stick by the person leading the group to draw attention to it. A variety of alternative ways for impressing the young who had joined in for the first time, such as turning them upside down and gently hitting their heads on the ground nearby, developed over the years. As the manors were organised into church parishes so the tradition followed the parish boundary. Today the church boundary does not always conform to the civil boundary, nor indeed the welter of other areas into which the countryside has since been divided.

The earliest reference to beating the bounds in Peter Tavy was found in the 'Parish Book', held by Mr Parsons Crossing of Langsford, where an account of the bounds being beaten on 26 September 1791 was said to be recorded. Unfortunately this book has been lost. Further references tell us that the bounds were beaten in 1867, 1873 and 1878, and no doubt intermittently since the earlier date. A full account of the bounds was made in 1882 when, on 3 June, the rector, Revd J.F. Bryant, representatives of the Dukes of Cornwall and Bedford with George Palmer (Godsworthy), Peter Holmes (Harragrove), John Doidge (Coxtor), John G. Bray (Wisdom), Thomas Prout (opposite the inn), William J. Fuge, Joseph Rowe, John Peek and William Jordan Dodd set out from the confluence of the Peter Tavy Brook with the River Tavy. Skirting the manor of Cudlipptown they climbed up Smearn Down to Boulders Tor (sic), then followed the moor lane to Stephen's Grave, over Lanson Moor to Jaddy Grip and onwards to the River Walkham, where they stopped for refreshment. They then followed the right bank of the river, casting a stone into the water to claim half the river, as far as Hanging Stone. Here they turned on the boundary of Shilla Parks to arrive at a 'new' bound stone to be marked on the Picket Rock. They continued across to the head of Blackamoor Coombe to Doghill, then by Colyton Lane to Glanville Meadow and by the right hedge they reached the parish stone on the Moorshop road. They then followed that road back to Harford Bridge. This itinerary is significantly different from the old church parish boundary, which, after skirting Cudlipptown, traced the boundary to include Willsworthy as far as Beardon before turning east to Didlake Foot, then south towards the source of the Walkham, which it followed to Shilla Parks.

The bounds were again beaten in 1892 and 1897. After a lapse of 25 years the tradition was revived in 1923, when it is said that the health of King George V was drunk to musical accompaniment at 'Longbettor Hedge', and three ladies accompanied the men for the first time; they were Mrs Loftus Dodd, who had come down especially from Bath, Mrs Hannah Ash and Mrs Arthur Sleeman. On that occasion much the same route was taken as in 1882. However, since then various courses have been taken in 1927, 1932, 1951, 1962, 1970, 1982 and 1992. Several of these beat only the bounds of the old manor of Peter Tavy, which excluded the further reaches of the moor above Willsworthy and returned above the Walkham, excluding Pitts Cleave and Harford Bridge. In the year 2000 to celebrate the millennium, the whole perimeter of 35 miles was beaten to include Cudlipptown, Willsworthy and the outlying farms south of Beardon and Bearwalls, before turning west to return along the River Walkham and down Collaton Lane out to Moorshop, before turning along the old Tavistock road to include Pitts Cleave and Harford Bridge.

The lord of the manor of Cudlipptown at the time of writing, John E. Kempe, still asserts his right to beat the bounds of the manor and this has been accomplished regularly since 1948 (see section on Cudlipptown, the Hamlets & Sortridge).

The ladies prepare to join the 'Beating of the Bounds' in 1994. Left to right; Ivy Dodd, William & Timothy Dodd, Jane Ball, Phyllis Dodd, James Perkins at the back with Ida Lynd, Katherine Haine, Dorothy Maunder.

The scene above Willsworthy during the 'beating of the bounds', 1932. Note the horses used in those days.
It is believed that the gentleman in breeches and a white coat was Colonel Worskett who lived at Baggator.

DEVON TO WIT.

PARISH OF PETERTAVY.

NOTICE

IS HEREBY GIVEN to the several Lords of Manors, Landholders, and Persons entitled to Rights of Common, in, and adjoining the said Parish, that we, the undersigned Parish Officers of Petertavy, with the Inhabitants thereof, will proceed to perambulate and view the Boundaries of the said Parish, on the

THIRD DAY OF JUNE NEXT,

When and where all Persons interested, may attend and be present at such view, which will begin at the village of Petertavy, at Ten o'clock in the Morning.

GEORGE PALMER, *Churchwarden.*
PETER HOLMES, *Overseer.*

Dated Petertavy, 19th May, 1882.

Tavistock Printing Company, Limited, Bedford Square, Tavistock.

Notices, like this one from 1882, were put up in several places around the parish to warn
people of the coming 'beating of the bounds'.

Above: *Revd Pratt in deep conversation at Stephen's Grave, the piece of upright granite in the centre front of the picture, 1932.*

Left: *'Beating the bounds', 1990. Left to right: Bill Dodd, James Perkins, ?, Ken Ball, Cyril Abel, Graham Collins; front right: John Douglas.*

Lunch on the 1932 'beating of the bounds'. Note the barrel of water!

The sack race.

The obstacle race.

The wheelbarrow race.

Above: *Children in the sack races, part of the sports at the Queen's Silver Jubilee, 1977.*

Top right: *The entrance to the school decorated for the Coronation of King George V in 1937.*

Right: *Bryan Rowse, Bill Dodd and Ken Ball plant the commemorative Jubilee 'conker' tree on Smeardon Down, June 1977.*

Left: *Celebrating the Coronation of King George V, this small cup with the King and Queen Mary's portraits was also sold as a present to remember the village.*

Below: *This rather more conventional cup is a simple reminder of the village and was produced at the Silver Jubilee (1935).*

Left: *The tradition continues with this Millennium mug that was presented by the Parish Council to all children in the parish who were under the age of 16 on millennium day, 1 January 2000.*

The Coombe and the Clam as they were in 1900, a rocky wilderness through which the villagers working at Merrivale and beyond would trudge back and forth to work.

Below: *Heather Gregory, Gillian Rice and Wendy Greening enjoy a swim in the pool in the Coombe, c.1933. Note the square changing hut in the background.*

Above: *Even rubber boats were used in the pond.*

The reopening of the swimming pool in the Coombe in 1933.

The Coombe

Peter Tavy Coombe has attracted artists over many years, although it has changed significantly in the twentieth century. It bears the Colley, or as it was known until recent years, the Peter Tavy Brook, from its source in the shallow valley above Wedlake down to the village itself where the brook joins the Tavy. At its deepest point, Great Coombe Tor rises on its southern bank with Little Coombe Tor to the north. Early pictures show that until the last 60 or 70 years it was a barren, rock-strewn valley with tumbling waters, quiet pools and small waterfalls. In its lower reaches, the old mill leat in front of Coombe Cottages runs upriver from Higher Mill to Southditch, where the Clam crosses to the southern bank; all now shrouded in trees and bushes. Footpaths give a choice of climbing the heights of Great Coombe Tor or a more gentle walk to the pool and along the brook to confront the tor from the east.

Early in the twentieth century, and doubtless for years before, villagers swam in the many pools during the hot summers. As the days of the grist-mills came to an end before the First World War the old millpond opposite Southditch Cottage fell into disrepair and was drained. An area on the opposite bank and above the Clam, which flooded when the brook was in spate and may have been used to supplement the water for the mills in dry summers, was converted to a small pool for swimmers.

In turn this fell into disuse due to the war and it was not until 1933 that the village sports committee decided to build an open-air swimming pool for the village on what was believed to be common land. The Hoare Brothers donated stone from their quarry at Pitts Cleave and villagers supplied the labour force. The total cost for materials and labour reached £33.7s.6d. A pit some six feet deep was cleared and the walls built. A corrugated-iron shed was erected as a changing room and the pool was opened with due celebration.

After the Second World War, when again the pool was in need of repair, it had been discovered that the land and pond belonged to the Duchy of Cornwall. In 1949 an agreement was drawn up between the village sports committee and the Duchy, which allowed for a pond with a concrete base and dressing sheds to be constructed at a premium of five shillings a year. Little was done, however, and the sports committee disappeared within a few years. This time the Parish Council took it on, re-negotiating the agreement and setting up a leisure committee. Temporary measures were taken and the pool came back into use. By 1991, however, the laws of health and safety had changed and questions of public liability arose. After much discussion the Parish Council found enough money for its restoration as a wildlife pond, with grants from the Duchy, the Community Council of Devon, British Telecom and National Power, as well as the efforts of villagers. The Council agreed that work should begin. A total of 50 tons of concrete were carried across fields and over hedges, so that a 100mm base could be laid inside a day. The pond was not for swimming, indeed a notice was provided saying so, together with a lifebelt for the unmindful. Work to point the walls and replace loose stone, together with the addition of a 150mm pipe and valve to drain the pool over winter, were all completed in time for the opening barbecue in September 1994.

The pond is not the only site in the Coombe to have a history, as the Clam below Southditch Cottage also had to survive the torrents that came down the brook when heavy rains fell on the moor above. The floods in 1891 washed it away and brought many a rock down the river. A lady looking up the Coombe just minutes before recounted how it looked as if a wall of water was rushing towards the village, and so it was. Small shippens were washed away and low-lying farms at Churchtown and Harford flooded to upper window level.

Jessie Cole (née Bellamy) who was a churchwarden for 38 years from 1951–89.

John Vogwill was a churchwarden for 20 years between 1923–43 and Chairman of the Parish Council from 1967–70. He also served on the Rural District Council.

Parish Councillors, 1990. The Parish Councillors leading the 'beating of the bounds'.
Left to right: Esme Wheeler, Kenneth Ball, John Douglas, William (Bill) Dodd, Geoffrey Porter, Ann Cole (Clerk); seated: Bryan Rowse (Chairman).

The Parish Council

During the fifteenth and sixteenth centuries there was a gradual transference of the powers of lords of the manor to what was called the 'Vestry'. This name arose simply because the parishioners that elected the body usually met in a room called the vestry, near or attached to the church and normally used by priests and others to robe for services. By custom, the Church of England incumbent was the Chairman, whilst a smaller number of the rate-paying parishioners formed a select Vestry to administer the affairs of the parish. The so-called 'open Vestry' was held annually when the select Vestry would be elected. Before the Reformation of 1539 the nave and porch of the church were used for public meetings of all sorts, the chancel remaining as the holy part of the church and under the strict supervision of the priest. It is perhaps surprising that so far no evidence of the medieval use of St Peter's in this way has emerged, but it seems likely that the north side of the churchyard was used for fayres and markets. As late as 1870

there is a report of a small fayre being held on the second Wednesday of each month at Peter Tavy. After the Reformation, what is now Church Cottages was built to accommodate the brewhouse and provide a space for the feasts after church festivals, the nave being filled with pews for the first time.

It was the responsibility of the Vestry to appoint the parish constable and the necessary officers to set and collect the rates for the poor, the highways and the church. There are very few records of the appointment of constables in Peter Tavy. Although five names were put forward in 1854, there is no record that any were in fact appointed.

Even before the earliest Poor Law Acts of Henry VIII, the parishes were responsible for providing support to the sick, the old and the needy. At first, churchwardens were appointed at the annual Vestry meeting to see to this side of parish business. William Burgess was such a man in 1553, followed by William Burne and John Glubb the younger, in 1572. The role

Peter Tavy 'Worthies' (also titled Parish Council, 1919). This picture contains too many people to be just a picture of the Parish Council, but was so titled and suggests that other 'Worthies' were invited. Some of the true Council for that date are missing. Left to right, back row: *John Holmes, William Rowse, Frank Littlejohns, ? Gill (or Giles), Edward F. Dodd, John Isaac Hill (Kingsett);* front row: *Walter Holmes, William Milman, George H. Abel, Thomas Roskilly, Harry Reep.*

continues to the present day. Although many only held the post for three to four years, in the last century George Abel was churchwarden for 17 years, John Vogwill for 20 years, and Jessie Cole (née Bellamy) broke all records with a stay of 38 years.

The need for a separate poorhouse in Church Cottages disappeared when the workhouse at Tavistock was built to serve all the merged parishes of the Tavistock Union formed in the 1830s. The Union Board of Guardians was made up of elected members from the parishes and the Revds Bryant and Lester served on the board as did Henry Spry of Sortridge in 1866 and Peter Holmes of Harragrove in 1864. The School Board had been similarly formed and parish members appointed; again it would fall to the incumbent to represent the parish, but by 1904 Harry Reep and John Howe of Hilltown represented Hillbridge School with Charles Mudge of Wappisworthy (Wapsworthy) and William Palmer of Redeford being nominated for Peter Tavy School. Overseers were also appointed to assist with the supervision of the Poor Law aspects of the church-wardens' role. Peter Holmes, John Arthur Reep, Thomas G. Bray and John G. Bray held these posts in 1880, with John Holmes being the collector of rates and assistant overseer. It was also necessary to appoint a separate collector for the Central Government's taxes, and Peter Holmes and George Palmer undertook the job at the time. In 1883 William Williams took over from George Palmer but otherwise the officers remained the same until 1885. That year saw Henry Reddicliffe and James Cole replace Peter Holmes and Thomas Bray, with John Doidge and William Williams as land- and income-tax collectors. William Harvie replaced William Williams the following year and in 1888 John Arthur took over from John Doidge. This seems to have been the quiet period before the storm. In March 1889 it was announced that:

The Vestry considering the remuneration by way of poundage sufficient for collecting the Land and Income Taxes and no resident being willing to undertake it, have considered it best not to make any appointment in the matter.

In May of the same year:

The assistant overseers to apply to the Magistrates for an Order to eject Elizabeth Gilbert from the house belong-ing to the Parish which she now occupies, she having failed to comply with due notice from the parish officers.

Later the same month it was stated that: 'The Vestry do not recommend the purchase of a Steam Roller for the Tavistock Highway District.' And in October 1889: 'The basis for the County Council (rate) be not

appealed against but the Vestry wants more informa-tion on the Income Tax of other parishes.' No appointment to assess and collect taxes was made again in 1890–92. However, in 1893 T.M. Rogers of Cudlipptown and William Harvie of Will Farm were appointed. As a final flourish of their independence, slight as it was, the Vestry asked the Board of Guardians and Local Government Board to sever the parish of Calstock from the Tavistock Union and place it with Cornwall.

In 1894 the Local Government Act transferred most of their responsibilities to civil parish councils. From now on the Civil Parish Council took control. Five of the seven members were previously on the Vestry, including the Chairman. The names of the councillors of the first Civil Council were:

Revd Francis John Bryant, The Rectory,
    Peter Tavy, Chairman
George Henry Abel, North Godsworthy,
    Vice Chairman
Edward Dodd, the Village
Peter Holmes, Coxtor
Thomas Martin Rogers, Cudlipptown
John Reddicliffe, Wappisworthy (Wapsworthy)
William Harvie, Will Farm

The Parochial Church Council in Peter Tavy disappeared until 1921 when, after a period in which the incumbent was left to run the parish on his own, it was decided that some measure of the parish-ioners' interests should be reinstated. Today, civil parish councils in the area continue to bear responsi-bility for parish-owned property, some of the local highways, and in advising the councils of West Devon Borough Council and the National Park Authority.

The work of the Clerk to the old Church Council had originated in the need of the lord of the manor to be represented in each church of his manors and to collect the tithes. In medieval times he might very well be a priest in minor orders, although as early as the thirteenth century the Archbishop of Canterbury had to forbid the appointment of two priests in any one parish. This led to non-priest appointments and gradually to regulations as to which persons were eligible. According to a minute in the St Peter's records in 1820:

Clerks must be 20 years or older and known to be honest and sufficient in reading, writing and a competent singer. The said to have the ancient wage without diminution by the churchwardens.

With the arrival of the civil councils the work of the Clerk escalated and it is now an important position in local government at the parish level.

Church Parish Clerks

No record of the names prior to 1809 has been found. Most records seem to have been made by the rector before about that time.

1809	*Richard WILLIAMS*
1812–22	*William BURLEY*
1822	*James BOULTER*
1852–73	*William PALMER*
1878–94	*James Fuge DODD (also held the post of Sexton)*

There was no Parochial Church Council until 1921.

1921–71	*Mrs Francis SLEEMAN*
1971–98	*Mrs Kathleen SIMMONS*
1998–	*Patrick CASHELL*

Clerks to the Civil Parish Council

1894–1902	*John HOLMES*
1902–30	*William WILLIAMS*
1930–60	*Arthur J. SLEEMAN*
1960–73	*Ray DOWNTON*
1973–77	*Michael GUEST*
1977–79	*Jane BALL*
1979–83	*Barbara BUTTERFIELD*
1983–87	*Linda WEBB*
1987–88	*Sylvia SANKEY*
1988–89	*Suzanne PHILLPOTT*
1989 (Mar–Sept)	*Mrs WOLFSON*
1989–	*Ann COLE*

George Henry Abel was a churchwarden for 17 years from 1902–19 and an overseer for the Council from 1907–18. He took over the Chairmanship of the Council after many years as Vice Chairman when Revd Bryant died in 1908, and remained in office until 1919.

Parish Council, 1949. Left to right: Arthur Sleeman, William Henry Bellamy, Albert Bellamy, Revd Brian Pratt, William Frederick Dodd, John Vogwill, Henry Stevens, Bertram Cole.

Church Cottages

Church Cottages are amongst the oldest existing buildings in the village and probably date to the sixteenth century. They were built to hold the church festivals and provide stabling for those riding to the church from more distant farms. In many parishes, in addition to holding the right to brew ale, the lord of the manor provided church houses and a welcome income that was held in common with the tenants of the manor. The upper hall, which was used for meetings and feasts, had below it a brewery and a kitchen. In Peter Tavy the entrance was by means of a narrow passage from Church Hill to a doorway, which can still be seen, on the churchyard side of the building. This entrance was blocked up in 1825 on the instructions of the Archdeacon of Plymouth who happened to be visiting when a man, the worse for drink, was found lying in the passageway. It must have been at this date that the new entrance to the house was built at the west end, facing the Green. An early Census in 1791 reported a village population of 232 living in 47 houses, and identified 12 of them as being paupers. Although the parish had been responsible for those 'who were sick and unable to work' since the time of Henry VIII, it is probable that this would have been the first call on the parish to provide actual accommodation, and the lower floor of Church Cottages was put to this use. In 1813 the Vestry provided some educational help and it is likely that a school was being held in the hall above the paupers' rooms, for it is not until 1823 that the 'turf' school was built at the west end of the cottages. By 1865 the Church House had been converted into two cottages and the hall divided to provide an upper storey for the tenants, but the cost of maintenance and the low rental led the Vestry to offer them for sale. There were no takers and one was finally let to a Mrs Phillips for £1 per year, the other was let to John Shambrooke, the church sexton. In 1876 the Vestry, holding no hope of a sale, paid for the repair of a chimney and a door.

The east end of the cottages remained as stables until 1986, though seldom used for horses in the later years. The small stone shed along the roadway provided the necessary toilet for the cottages and the hall above until more extensive alterations were made, incorporating the stable and providing three cottages with internal toilets. The building and gardens in front, still under the control of the Church authorities, were passed over to the Civil Parish Council in 1974.

The School, Peter Tavy

In 1839 the village school was held in a 'turf' building alongside Church Cottages, occupying the space where the Village Cross now stands opposite the Village Green, which lay between the houses of Richard Williams and James Ware. This school building was put up in 1823, with the cost of £30 being paid largely by the Duke of Bedford. Annual subscriptions from the Duke were supplemented by a regular contribution from parents to pay the running expenses.

There is some evidence of an earlier school started by Revd John Jago as early as 1750, which probably met in the upstairs room of what is now Church Cottages. In 1813 the minutes of the Vestry meeting record the purchase of a copy of Dr Bell's *System of Education* at a cost of two shillings, but there is no record of a teacher at the school before 1823.

Extra space was certainly needed by 1857 when the school roll shows some 70 pupils attending. It was probably this rising population that provided the stimulus to approach the Duke of Bedford for the land and money to build a new school. In 1859 the Duke conveyed the site, on which the present Village Hall stands, to the rector and Parochial Church Council on the understanding that it would be conducted under the principles of the National Society. The committee which was formed to run the school comprised the rector, Revd Thomas Gibbons (chairman), Parsons Crossing, John Arthur, William Doidge, Thomas Watkins, William Spear and Peter Holmes. The site was part of the Duke's estate in the manor of Peter

Peter Tavy School, 1896. Left to right, back row: *Lily Doidge, A. Nankivell, Lily Edwards, Florrie Perkins, Laura Milman, Arthur Sleeman, Walter Phillips;* middle row: *Tom Vogwill, Frank Doidge, Eadie Littlejohns, Liza Phillips, Eadie Doidge, William Nankivell;* front row: *Ada Rich, Rhoda Rich, Bert Hicks, George Littlejohns, Jim Nankivell, Annie Littlejohns, Florrie Edwards. The school mistress on the left is Mrs White and on the right is Mrs Rowe.*

Tavy and was previously a garden for a large house, which stood on land between the present hall and chapel. It is a mystery why the building work took so long, for it was not until 1865 that the school was opened and then only for girls and infants. The boys had to attend the 'old school' and continued to do so until 1870, when the Parochial Church Council decided to take the old 'turf' building down 'to give a better sight of the church from the village'.

Although local and national education authorities increasingly imposed their rules on building standards and suitable accommodation for teaching, the extension now used as a kitchen was not built until 1926, when £106 was collected in the village to do the work and provide more space. The outside toilets were an early requirement. Betty Wilton (née Leetoose) remembers the girls leaving by a door at the back of the hall, which looked out on to a grass play area, to reach their toilet, whilst the boys left by the front door, going across the hard playground to reach their toilet, which was back to back with the girls' and divided from them by a high wall. There was no flush system and just two buckets in each place. Similarly, when James Perkins was at school, during school breaks the girls played on the grass area that had flower beds and the boys played on the tarmac below. The lobby at the old doorway was used to hang coats and Miss Milman's room was straight ahead, whilst Mrs Sleeman had the large hall for the older children. In each room there was a large picture on the wall; in Mrs Sleeman's room it was 'Jesus knocking on the door – the light of the world' by Holman Hunt, and in the smaller room was a picture of Jesus with his arms around children of different races. Food was not

provided and after a breakfast of a boiled egg and a hunk of bread smothered with treacle and cream, Betty took sandwiches to school and crossed over the road to her aunt, Mrs Stratford at Jasmine Cottage, to eat them at lunch time. The kitchen was not built until after the First World War when the authorities started bringing hot dinners to the school.

A single stove provided heating in the larger room and a small open fireplace was used in the small room. When necessary, lighting was provided by oil lamps until the mid 1930s, some time after electricity had reached the village. The church records for 1933 explain how £35 could be borrowed from the school fund to heat the church by electricity whilst withholding it from the school. That decision was rescinded within weeks but electricity still did not come to the school until 1937, with the proviso that 'a definite body shall be named as responsible for the upkeep so that no expense shall fall upon the church.'

Under the 1902 Act the school had come under the Local Education Authority as a Voluntary Church School, under the governance of a board of management always chaired by the current rector. Revd Pratt took assembly on Monday and Tuesday with a scripture lesson for one or other of the classes afterwards, otherwise Mrs Sleeman took it. In earlier times Revd Lester would attend every morning for assembly. Phyllis Dodd recalls that the girls were taught sewing and knitting, whilst the boys did woodwork. During the war there were so many evacuees that the large room was divided into two with a curtain and another teacher used to come to help. After the Second World War, parent/teacher organisations were being developed and that in Peter Tavy met nearly every

Peter Tavy School, 1906. Included in the picture are Mrs Susan Cole and the two boys standing in the centre are Frederick William Dodd and his brother, Loftus. It is probable that the lady on the right is Miss Milman.

Peter Tavy School, 1911.
Frances Docking is standing on the left, later to become Mrs Sleeman. Mary Milman is standing on the right.

week on a Tuesday, but seldom discussed much to do with the school as it was all common knowledge. The time was taken up playing cards; the teacher Miss Hosking seldom came as she felt she had little to add to what was already known. Wednesday evening was folk-dancing evening and Thursday evening was for the youth club. This was started by the Methodists and usually run by someone from the chapel. Sunday afternoon was time for Sunday School, generally held at the rectory for Church-of-England children by Mrs Lucy Pratt, the rector's wife.

Eileen Duncan recalls Mrs Sleeman – everybody called her Fanny but she expected to be called Frances – as an old-fashioned lady who was very meticulous with money. If she missed the bus to go into market at Tavistock she would prefer to wait for the next one some two hours later, rather than take a taxi. Everything was spotless in her bungalow in Harragrove Lane, especially the lino on the floor, but she had a great sense of humour and would always take part in the village fête, when she would tell your fortune from the playing cards.

Jan Lightfoot lived at Will Farm during the Second World War and had to walk to school at first. After a few weeks a taxi, driven by Syd Thomas from the inn, was arranged and the children piled into one

car. When they came to the hill at Hillbridge they had to get out and walk to the top, as the car could not manage with all of them on board. Peggy Stephens recalls that before the war Bert Cole ran the taxi service and it stopped for children at Wapsworthy, Hillbridge or Will Farm on a weekly rotation. They had to walk to the appropriate stopping place to meet his taxi. After a few months, when evacuees had swollen the numbers, the school at Hillbridge was opened and they had to walk there.

It is not surprising that attendance at school was not always at its best. Severe weather and illness were certainly causes of absence, but harvest, market day and wortleberry picking with other calls of the farm played their part. Soon after the war in 1946 the seniors were transferred to Tavistock and the school at Peter Tavy became solely a primary school. In 1959 the school was closed and the children transferred to Mary Tavy School, with some going to Tavistock.

In the original lease granted by the Duke of Bedford, his wily steward had written the words, 'for ever for the children and adults of the labouring, manufacturing, and poorer classes... and for no other purpose.' When the school closed in 1959 the building and land reverted to the Bedford family estates.

Peter Tavy School, 1927. Left to right, back row: *Mrs Sleeman, Bill Rice, Ronald Worth, Tom Friend, Alfred Wheaten, George Mudge, John Mudge, Ernest Duke, Leslie Rice, Ada Mudge, Miss Milman;* third row: *Amy Williams, Lily Mudge, Ivy Rice, Annie Down, Edna Mudge, May Williams, Sybil Friend, Beatrice Martin, Ida Williams, Lily Moyse, Doris Bisset, Betty Sillick;* second row: *Joyce Thomas, Dorothy Ballard, Freda Harris, Freda Williams, Joyce Miles, Gertrude Reed, Martha Mudge, May Carr, Kharmis Ball;* front row: *Charlie Mudge, Bob Sellick, Edwin Cooper, George Rooke, Ted Ballard, Fred Rice, Jack Bisset, Arthur Thomas, Peter Thomas.*

Schoolteachers at Peter Tavy School

1823	Grace CROKER
1857	Miss DREWE
1861	Amelia PORRELL
	Mrs (Elizabeth) WARE seems to have helped out until at least 1891
1865	Miss AXFORD
1870	Amelia JOLLY
1871	Miss M. PROUT
1872	Mr ROWE with Mrs ROWE to oversee needlework, she later taught the juniors for some years.
1873	Mrs WEBB as a temporary teacher soon followed by
1873–78	Susan CHAPPELL
1878	Sara HUGHES
1889–1909	Susan Jane COLE and Mrs WHITE
1902–43	Mary Helen MILMAN for the infants

She was suspended for three years whilst she obtained her teaching certificate and Annie Mudge, only 14 yrs old, took over.

This was not unusual as the school was based on a 'monitor' system by which the older children were expected to assist with the teaching of the younger ones.

1910	Frances DOCKING, to become Mrs Arthur SLEEMAN in 1919.

In 1923, because of falling numbers at the school, she was made redundant, but re-employed in 1927 and remained until 1943.

1941	Miss EVERY
1943	Doris BOWHAY for the infants. Mrs PENNY and Thelma WOOD, who was the last to work with Mrs Sleeman.
1943–59	Miss HOSKING

During the war, as the numbers of children rose with evacuees, a curtain was hung across the hall and supplementary teachers came to help.

Peter Tavy School, 1959. Left to right, back row: *Douglas Saye, Christopher Rich, Alan DeQuick, Gary Metters, Philip Sellick, Miss Hoskins;* middle row: *Sylvia Collins, Linda Greening, Angela Collins, Sylvia Saye, Karen Roberts;* front row: *David Jeffery, David Henderson-Howard, David Arscott, Nigel DeQuick. These were the last children to attend the school before it was closed.*

Hillbridge School

Many of the outlying farms and hamlets of the parish lie some way from the village school, and some children were evidently receiving little education. This concerned the managers, who in 1872 decided to provide a school at Hillbridge for those children at farms in the northern moor such as Standon, Gnattor, Baggator and Willsworthy. They decided to locate the school in the chapel of ease at Hillbridge where, apart from a Sunday service attended only four times a year by the rector himself and perhaps a social event on occasion, nothing took place. It was a grim place, with a stone floor and no heating or lighting, and a wooden floor was not put in until 1909. When heating was put in the coal had to be stored in the classroom. It was expected that the new school would provide for about 40 children if all attended, and they appointed Susannah Cole as the mistress with some assistance from Maria Geake. There were early difficulties in administering the school from the village and a separate committee was appointed to run it, but still under the chairmanship of the rector. To cover the expenses a fee of one penny per week was charged for the younger children, rising to two pennies per week for

the older ones. By 1905 the committee under the rector's chairmanship was Messrs Reep, Williams, Harvie, Holmes and Mudge. All was not well and reports indicate that the children were well behind in their learning. There was little in the way of equipment and until desks and books arrived in 1905 little progress seems to have been made. The following year Mrs Elizabeth Ladd was appointed mistress and she remained until 1924, during which time she lived and brought up her children at Wapsworthy. Life was not easy but a marked improvement was reported by the inspectors in 1910, which is surprising as the school roll had risen by this time to 62 and the age range was from 3 to 12 or even 14 .

During the First World War, on Friday and Saturday evenings, there were concerts and charity shows at the school, some being put on by the children, others by the adults. Dingle Weeks used to play the accordion for them.

By the early 1920s the roll had dropped to less than ten and it was decided that the school should close. Mrs Ladd was given short notice and by the spring of 1924 the school had shut.

Hillbridge School, c.1911. The teacher who is seated is thought to be Miss Ann Prescott (?).

However, the influx of evacuees at the start of the Second World War caused severe overcrowding at Peter Tavy and Hillbridge was reopened. Although a Miss Every was the first mistress at the reopened school, she lasted only a few days and before Christmas 1941 Miss Kathleen Taylor was appointed. She taught throughout the next five years single-handedly with classes sometimes up to 40 in number. At this time Revd Brian Pratt was the rector and took religious classes once or twice a month at the school. He had a small two-seater sports car with space behind the seats and children were given rides to the other side of the bridge. They then had to walk back!

The end of the war saw the evacuees return to their homes and the need for the school disappeared. It was closed in 1946. Mr Palmer, a butcher in

Schoolteachers at Hillbridge School	
1872	Mrs Susannah COLE
1872	Miss Maria GEAKE
1902	Miss Ann PRESCOTT
1906–24	Mrs Elizabeth LADD
1941	Miss EVERY
1941–46	Miss Kathleen TAYLOR

Tavistock, bought the building and turned it into a holiday residence, installing electricity for the first time. In 1974 he sold it and major alterations were undertaken to make it into a two-storey house.

The Village Hall

Steve Carreck

The school building had always been central to village life, used for social gatherings and special events and occasions. The Parish Council met there, concerts, shows and plays were performed, harvest teas held and even the Peter Tavy Ladies Choir practised there when they won the Tavistock area music competition in 1927! During the Second World War, the hall served as the meeting-place for the local Home Guard Platoon. It was also the venue for the popular Peter Tavy dances. Life-long village resident, James Perkins, remembered how people rode to the dances at the Village Hall, leaving their horses in the barns at Gatehouse Farm (his home) and Higher Churchtown, where the men would change into smart clothes. He recalled how, as a boy, he would lie in bed and hear them returning to collect their horses after the dances. Over 100 people would arrive to dance to a band playing the accordion, piano and drums. When he was older and attended the dances himself, he remembered paying an admission charge of 1s.6d. but a cup of tea, served in the small classroom, was extra!

When the school closed in 1959, a group of villagers gathered the following summer to create a Trust in which the Bedford Estate vested the property and land. The Trust stipulated that several matters were subject to any future decisions that might be made by the Minister of Education! But the building needed a great deal of work and redecoration before it could be used.

A committee of management was formed, the first chairman being George Medland. There was a fund-raising drive, fêtes were held in the grounds of the hall, and Eileen Abel remembers the barn dances held at Godsworthy and Sowtontown, which raised as much as £350 on some occasions. It was stipulated that the management committee should comprise two representatives each from the youth club, the Parent Teachers Association (who had met in the school hall on Tuesday evenings) and the Parochial Church Council, with up to eight additional elected members.

The youth club was perhaps originally formed to give an alternative to meeting at the big 'Barn's Door'

Peter Tavy Dramatic Society, c.1920. Left to right, back row: *Maud Smale, Frances Sleeman, John Vogwill, D. Giles, Durrie Blythe, Richard Fraser, Mrs Payne, ?, Jessie Bellamy, William Smale, William Reed;* centre: *Dorothy Edwards, Emily Hill, Leonora Fraser, Revd Austin Lester, Mrs Lester, Mrs Holmes, Mrs Vogwill, Miss French-Smith;* front row: *Peter Holmes, H. Fraser, Betty Lester, May Smale, Cecil Rice.*

at Gatehouse Farm – Mrs May Wakeham remembers the graffiti that was often scribbled on the walls by the youngsters gathering there. It continued to be very active, but the Parent Teacher Association collapsed without the focus of a school in the village. However, perhaps not surprisingly, the parents continued to meet in the hall as a bridge club!

By the early 1980s it became clear that the building needed more radical attention. The roof was leaking and paint peeling off the walls. An estimate of £6,000 was obtained for roof repairs and a group of unemployed teenagers, working under the 'Pathfinder Initiative', came to the village and decorated the back room at the cost of materials. Over £2,000 was raised by various events, but there was still a long way to go.

It is not known what brought the *Daily Mirror* to choose Peter Tavy in 1984 for an experiment into the effect of stopping television viewing for a week, but the 'Great Switch-Off' won widespread support in the village. Eileen Duncan recalls how Jessie Bellamy welcomed the idea, saying it would get everyone talking together again, not sitting in silence staring at the screen. But when asked how she would cope, her friend Ida Lynd replied, 'Oh, I shall be all right – I've got my gramophone!' The village's achievement was recognised with a visit by celebrity Jimmy Savile to switch the television back on. When it was all over, the newspaper donated £1,000 to the Village Hall's appeal and gave a colour television set, which was raffled by the hall committee to raise a further £323.

In recent years, the hall has continued to be at the centre of village activities. The annual 'Summer Fayre' – a joint project by hall, church and chapel – remains popular with residents and surrounding villagers alike. Held in the hall and its grounds, it spreads on into the chapel and grounds. In addition to private parties, village dances are still held here and there are regular meetings of the bridge club, the local spinners and weavers group and even Scottish country dancers! Shows continue to be staged there – recently under the auspices of the 'Villages in Action' scheme, bringing professional performers to rural communities.

In recent years, a new generation of the Village Hall Management Committee once again actively took up the challenge of refurbishing the building. After redecoration under the Community Service programme, more fundamental refurbishment was undertaken, financed partly by grant aid from the National Lottery, Community Council of Devon, West Devon Borough Council and partly by the Parish Council and the hall committee's fund-raising efforts. These include quiz nights, jumble sales and a 'Buy a Slate' campaign, under which donors are offered the prospect of entering Peter Tavy history if they could prove to have purchased the 'lucky slate', on which their name would be engraved for

Jimmy Savile turns on the TV, 1984.

1. Robin Armstrong, 2. Gary Metters, 3. Karl Reed,
4. 'Bill' Dodd, 5. Linda Butler, 6. Florrie Williams,
7. Lorraine Jeffery, 8. Gary Butler, 9. Jimmy Savile,
10. Noreen Lane. 11. Stephen Espin, 12. Linda Reed,
13. Clare (?) Windermere, 14. Heather Wyness,
15. Richard Windermere, 16. Terry Reed, 17. Barbara
Butterfield, 18. Kerry Reed, 19. Pat Porter, 20. ?

Youth club, 1966. Left to right: *Ruth Graham, Douglas Saye, Angela Collins, Sylvia Saye, Lesley Saunders, Marjorie Roberts, Enid Day, Philip Sillick, Sylvia Collins.*

Youth group, 1970s. Left to right: *Richard Ball, James Jeffery, Stephen Espin, Mark Watts, Tracey Watts, Janet Watts, Wendy Willcocks, Gillian Walter, Tracey Jeffery, Robert Gill, Gary Butler, Sally-Ann Gill.*

Minnows, 1998. Left to right: *1. Torie Abel,*
2. Megan Abel, 3. ?, 4. Sandra Dodd, 5. Rosalee Dodd, 6. Johanna Abel, 7. Alison Abel, 8. Bethany Abel,
9. Alice Upcott, 10. Sian Upcott, 11. Katherine Lewis, 12. Kimberley Upcott, 13. Camilla Lewis,
14. Paula Metters, 15. James Metters, 16. Sue Way, 17. Joseph Way, 18. Zoe Metters.

A birthday party at the Village Hall, 1983.

posterity! Works have already included the refurbishment of the dilapidated gents' toilet facilities to provide access for the disabled. It and the refurbished kitchen were re-roofed in Delabole slate to provide a weatherproof match with the remainder of the old school building.

Above: Back row, left to right: *Mark Watts, Tracey Jeffery, Karl Reed, Sally-Ann Gill, Naomi Pollard, Sandra Dodd, Laura Webb, Tracey Watts;*
middle row: *Emma Wyness, Stephen Espin, Janet Watts, Robert Gill, Gary Butler, Nick Friend;*
front row: *Kurt Reed, Andrew Friend, Celeste Pollard;*
far right: *Debbie Friend.*

Scottish country dancing, 2000.

Left to right: *Ann Cairns, Anne Donnelly, Jocelyn Watson, Angela Collins, James Watson, Derek Gdanitz, David Willans, Patrick Cashell, Dot Gdanitz, Mary Willans, John Bedford, Janet Bedford, Alison Watt, Mary-Ann Furze, Derek Rowe, Maire Gates, Barbara Howland, Peter Gates.*

Tramp of the Year, 1968. Fancy-dress competition to raise funds for the Village Hall.
Left to right: *James Medland (highly recommended), 'Tiny' Gait and Eric Gait (joint first), Sonia Morray (third place), David Hoatson (second place).*

St Peter's Church

There is no evidence of a Saxon church at Peter Tavy, however the Norman mask over the window of the south transept and the Norman priest door to the chancel suggest that at least by Norman times the church was in existence. Willsworthy, a Saxon manor within the parish of Peter Tavy, also has the remnants of an old chapel which is thought to have been used by mourners carrying their dead from the forest of Dartmoor to their Parish Church at Lydford. In 1384, 'Master David of Bagatorre' in the hamlet of Willsworthy was vicar of Tavistock and the small chapel at the side of Lych Way may have been for his private use. Various references to its use as a cow-shed occur in the last century and today no more than an 'ecclesiastical' window is to be found, high on the side of an old barn. The first reference to a priest at Peter Tavy is to 'Robert, chaplain of Tavi', c.1185. By 1270 Roger de Okston had been appointed for some years and, when raised to become Prebendary at St Teath in Cornwall, he held on to the parish of Peter Tavy until 1276, when Martin de Sheftesbyre was presented by the Priory at Plympton.

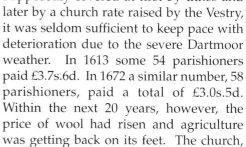

Many churches in Devon were rebuilt or enlarged in the episcopy of Bishop Grandisson, (1327–69) as a thanksgiving for deliverance after the famine years of 1317–20. It is probable that at St Peter's the chancel was rebuilt and the north and south transepts added around 1330, as these were the years when sheep farming was flourishing and agriculture had generally revived. The Black Death in 1348–50 brought the whole county to a standstill. Peter Tavy lost two, or possibly three, rectors during this period – a reflection of the number of villagers who must have died.

The next period of affluence, in the early-sixteenth century when wool was again making good prices, saw the rebuilding of the tower and the addition of the porch. In 1553 the Church Commissioners recorded that 'the Tower at Petrestavie contains three bells and the church plate consists of a silver chalice.' The church now consisted of a single nave with chancel, sanctuary and a tower at the west end with a full transept forming two side chapels. The next 100 years were times of turmoil in the Church and throughout the country, culminating in the Civil War. In Peter Tavy the picture is one of steady deterioration, with the rector, Andrew Gove, writing to the Registrar of the Bishop's Court at Exeter in 1673 in defence of a churchwarden. John Colbourne, the churchwarden accused of neglecting the church, had

Centre: The Norman mask is set in the wall above the window of the south transept and suggests the presence of a Norman church on this site.

been taken to the court by a parishioner who refused to pay the church rate. The sum was 1s.6d. but the rector wrote:

7th April 1673.
The reason hereof is John Colbourne an honest Churchwarden, your servant, on whom a (summonse) is served from the Consistory for his appearance there tomorrow. Pray assist him to your utmost... The church is neither wind nor watertight, and many woeful defrayments in and about it for want of money.
Your well wishing friend, Andrew GOVE

Maintenance of the church fabric has always been a problem. Supposedly covered at first by tithes and later by a church rate raised by the Vestry, it was seldom sufficient to keep pace with deterioration due to the severe Dartmoor weather. In 1613 some 54 parishioners paid £3.7s.6d. In 1672 a similar number, 58 parishioners, paid a total of £3.0s.5d. Within the next 20 years, however, the price of wool had risen and agriculture was getting back on its feet. The church, led by Revd Thomas Pocock, gained the north aisle in 1692 shortly after the churchyard had been enlarged northwards. The structure of the church has altered little since those days, though at some time, probably in the early 1700s, a gallery was added to the west end of the church, where a small village group played music for the services. Records show that in 1791 Richard Williams, the Parish Clerk, played the flute, George Mudge the hautboy, Edward Burley the violin and two others unnamed played the treble and bass viols. There was also a choir which was trained for nearly 50 years by George Mudge for an annual fee of £3.3s. There is no record of the removal of the gallery but it seems likely that it was taken down during the so-called Victorian 'renovations' of the 1870s, when the pews were replaced and the font moved back to its present position at the west end of the nave.

Many who knew Peter Tavy before 1983 will remember the lime trees that engulfed the whole churchyard. They had been planted in 1760, perhaps to commemorate the Coronation of George III, though there is a tale that they replaced a ring of oak trees that circled the church and restricted the enlargement of the churchyard at the end of the previous century. For more than 150 years the lime trees grew untouched, but in the early 1900s the minutes of the Council meeting record falling branches, requiring the removal of those around the south gate. After the First World War further complaints led to coppicing, which was repeated from time to time as required. When, in the 1970s, it seemed likely that

Watercolour of St Peter's Church, Peter Tavy, 1847. The artist is unknown.

further attention would be needed, expert opinion reported that all but two trees were rotting and dangerous. Such was the affection in the village for the trees that it was not until 1983 that they were finally felled and smaller, randomly-placed trees of limited growth were planted.

On 6 November 1803 the church tower was struck by lightning in a storm which is also said to have destroyed the Iron-Age fort on Whit Tor. The north-west pinnacle of the tower was 'thrown to the ground'; a large hole was made in the roof at the west end of the church above the gallery, which was also badly damaged. Several pews were splintered and the west door of the tower was blown out. Some repairs were instituted immediately, nevertheless it was some months before the stonework of the tower was replaced. An advertisement in the *Exeter Flying Post* for 18 April 1804 sought bids for the masonry to be repaired. When it was finally done the stone stairway to the roof of the tower was closed off at the level of the bell chamber to make a stronger support for that pinnacle, but it also blocked easy access to the tower roof.

During the incumbencies of Revds Thomas Pocock and William Macbean a great deal of change took place within the church and an account written in 1848 of a visit to the church makes interesting reading:

The approach to the church from the Village Green is by a wide garden gate, the church is completely surrounded by some forty lime trees, they are full grown and cast a heavy shadow in the summer. An avenue of these trees leads us to the Porch with its panelled ceiling and wooden bosses carved with foliage at the intersections.

Inside a staircase on our left leads to the gallery which fills the west end of the nave and where an harmonium rests. Beneath the gallery are pews with the ancient font standing in the archway to the north nave. To our right are more pews stretching towards the chancel. The frontmost of the pews are heavily carved with figures of Tudor date... The chancel is divided from the nave by a painted screen of the saints to the right of which is the rector's pew and a canopy that overhangs the part used for the sermon.

In 1866 the rector, the two churchwardens, Thomas Watkins and John Reep, with William Palmer, John Doidge, William Doidge, Henry Spry and Elias Bray were appointed by the Vestry to report to the next meeting on the renovation of the church. No report has been found and nothing was done until 1870 when the roof was tarred; Elias Bray, one of the village masons, replaced the floor and replastered the walls, and Thomas Blatchford, a village carpenter, replaced the pews.

In 1965 raised pine wood pews were removed from the south transept; they had been put upon an earth floor and had rotted. In the preparations for a new slate floor an alabaster figurine of an armoured knight was discovered buried with some human remains. The figurine, now in the museum at Plymouth, has been identified as a Nottingham plaque of the fourteenth century.

Renovations carried out in 1991 confirmed that a slit window, seen from outside, with a staircase to a rood loft and a hagioscope, or squint, had been closed up. A clay pipe dating from around 1650 was found in the squint, suggesting the date when this happened.

The Induction of Revd Brian Pratt, 1932. Left to right: *John Vogwill (churchwarden), Revd Brian Pratt, The Lord Bishop of Exeter, Revd H.C. Pratt (Brian's father) and the rector of Colebrook, George Abel (churchwarden).*

Below: *The medieval screen is part of a larger rood screen that divided the chancel from the rest of the nave. It was probably taken down during the Commonwealth years and stored until the restoration of the monarchy in 1660. By that time the staircase to the rood loft had been closed, as had the squint and other alterations to the chancel, so this painted screen with its partner were placed behind the altar. Whether from being damaged by people in earlier years drawing their fingers across a favourite saint, or more mundanely from the feet of clerics and cleaners when at the east end of the church, significant damage has been done. The two remaining panels are hung at the west of the north aisle.*

Above: *Inside the church in 1910. Note the old boiler flue where the pulpit now stands, and the Ten Commandments on panels each side of the altar. The church was lit by paraffin lamps and heating was achieved with a solid-fuel boiler at the front and back of the church.*

St Peter's Church traces its origins to at least Norman times. It has seen many changes but remains an oasis of peace towering over the village that takes its name. This picture shows part of the circle of lime trees that enclosed the churchyard from 1760 to 1983 when they were removed as all but a few suffered from rot in the trunks from unwise pollarding.

Bell-ringers, 1935.
Left to right: *?,*
William Cole, ?,
Frances Sleeman,
Lily Vogwill,
William Smale.

Bell-ringers, 1936. Left to right,
back row: *William Smale, ?, Leslie Ash,*
?, William Cole; front: *Hannah Ash*
(née Vogwill), Lily Vogwill (née Cole),
Frances Sleeman (née Docking).

Left: *The carved panels now hanging in the south*
transept were originally part of the front pews in the
nave. It has been suggested that they were the family
pews of either the Drake or the Cole families, both of
whom owned land in the parish. Carved in Tudor
times they portray mermaids and green men, with
pagan roots. Dismantled during the Victorian
renovations, they were fashioned together to form
a screen at the base of the tower. The door can be
seen with a keyhole, in the middle of the picture.
The modern tower screen was erected in 1975 and
the Tudor screen was removed to the south transept.

Church Bells

There have been bells in the tower at Peter Tavy certainly since 1553, when it was recorded by the Church Commissioners that there were 'Three bells and a Chalice'. The present bells number six, the oldest of which was cast in 1722. Further bells were recast in 1743, 1761 (this bell was recast in 1882), two in 1790, and the final bell in 1882. Apart from the war years of 1939–45 the bells had been rung regularly until 1989 when a major overhaul was required. This was completed in time for Christmas 1991. The record of tower captains is woefully inadequate and includes: William Cole, William Smale, Albert Maunder, John C. Bellamy, Arthur Bellamy, A. Sleeman, J. William Mudge and Norman Nankivell.

Some Recent Rectors

Revd F.J. Bryant. Rector, 1879–1907

The late Elsie Jeffery recalled Revd Francis Bryant as a tall, white-haired man who always walked through the village wearing his cassock and a black round, flat hat. He visited his parishioners regularly; especially during the week after he had noticed an absence from church the previous Sunday. His services were considered 'genial', perhaps from his habit of preaching extempore. The story is told of a friend who, after congratulating him on his sermon, remarked, 'it would have been all the better for some study in the week before'. The following week his friend told him that his sermon had improved markedly from the preparation he had taken. 'Oh!' he replied, 'maybe, but I forgot what I was supposed to preach about, so made it all up as I went along.' For some years he was on the Tavistock Board of Guardians and was known for his opposition to any increase in the salaries of Poor Law officers.

Revd A.S. Lester. Rector, 1908–32

A man who expected matters to be in a proper order, he was appalled at the state of the rectory when he arrived. He refused to live there until the new rectory, now Glebe House, had been built in 1911, under his close direction. He was an accomplished man who played several different musical instruments including the organ, which he would do before the service or if the organist was not available. He would give tuition to children he thought capable of entry into a grammar school and with his wife he ran a small school at Mary Tavy. His wife, whom he married soon after coming to Peter Tavy, was the organist at the church for many years and was the first lady to be elected to the position of churchwarden in 1921.

Bell-ringers, 2000. Left to right, back row: *Alison Carreck, Roger Meyrick, Steve Carreck, Martin Wheddon, Norman Nankivell (tower captain), Jill Morris, Jerry Morris;* front row: *Anna Dodd, Alan Sparks, Angela Collins.*

St. Peter Tavy Parish Church.

Dedication of the Organ ..

On WEDNESDAY. August 15th. 1906.

AT 11 A.M.
THE DEDICATION SERVICE.

The SERMON will be Preached by . . . . .

The Right Rev. The Bishop of St. Germans.

A Public Luncheon will be held in the Schoolroom at 12.30.

TICKETS 2/-.

AN ORGAN RECITAL

WITH   BY
Sacred Vocal Solos,   Mr. J. Tomlinson,
Will be given at 3 p.m.   Organist at the
                                      Parish Church, Tavistock.

The Tavistock Parish Church Choir will assist.

A PUBLIC TEA
will be held in the Schoolroom at 5 p.m.
Tickets 1/- Labourers of the Parish,
Church Choir, and Helpers, 6d.

AT 7 P.M.   Evening Prayer with a Sermon
By REV. E. CAREW BROWNE.

The Offerings at both Services will be devoted to the Organ Fund.

THE TAVISTOCK PRINTING COMPANY, LIMITED. TAVISTOCK.

View of St Peter's Church, looking north-west.

Revd B.C.C. Pratt. Rector, 1932–65

After a spell as curate at Tavistock, he had gone to be the vicar of Woburn, before returning to Devon. He was always very keen that the village youth should take part in every activity, including their attendance at church. As curate in Tavistock he had joined the local football team and rejoined them when he returned to Peter Tavy. He famously captained the village team (the Coombe Boys), in 1944 when they beat the Royal Marines on a pitch at Harford Bridge by three goals to two. He not only encouraged village activities but also took part in them all. Betty Wilton recalls that when she was a girl living at Standon she used to come down to the chapel at Hillbridge for Sunday School. When Revd Pratt was there he used to give the children rides in the boot of his three-wheeled car. He was popular with most people and helped his wife found the Mothers' Union with Mrs Walter Holmes in 1933. Brian Pratt was the last rector to live at the rectory, which was sold by the Church authorities soon after his death in 1965.

Left: *In 1821 a barrel organ was installed in the gallery at the back of the church. Known as 'the sounds to the glory' it was scarcely loud enough and restricted the range of hymns that could be sung. In 1846 an harmonium was added to the small orchestra that played there and in 1859 the first pipe organ was built at the east end of the church. By 1902 this organ was on its last legs and it was decided to have a full pipe organ, which was installed by John Guest of Exeter. The organ was not dedicated until 1906, as it took some time to raise the £150 required for it to be built.*

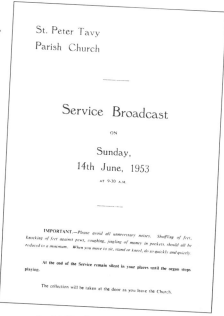

St. Peter Tavy
Parish Church

Service Broadcast

ON

Sunday,
14th June, 1953

AT 9.30 A.M.

IMPORTANT.—*Please avoid all unnecessary noises. Shuffling of feet, knocking of feet against pews, coughing, jingling of money in pockets, should all be reduced to a minimum. When you move to sit, stand or kneel, do so quickly and quietly.*

At the end of the Service remain silent in your places until the organ stops playing.

The collection will be taken at the door as you leave the Church.

The BBC came to Peter Tavy in 1953. It was a live broadcast to the nation and some in the village still remember the cables and the trucks involved. One or two stories have been told of how Revd Pratt told the choir that if he took out his handkerchief to wipe his nose during the last hymn, the last verse was to be repeated, as the service had ended a little early. All the instructions to the congregation are noted at the bottom of the leaflet.

The Churchyard at St Peter's Church

Since time immemorial people have been buried in graves in cemetery areas. The arrival of Christianity in Devon around AD600–700 drew these plots towards the church, with the most important villagers being buried to the east. Few, if any, stones marked the place and it was not until the early-seventeenth century that gravestones began to appear in the churchyard. The earliest memorial is within the church and marks the death of five daughters of Richard Evelegh, rector in 1632. Two small coffin-shaped stones to the east of the church may be their resting place. In the yard the earliest gravestone is that of Roger Cole, who died in 1663. Nearly 1,000 graves have been identified, though 180 remain unmarked, but the registers show that over 2,000 people have been buried here since 1620. The number of 'teardrop' stones between 1680 and 1720 showed the increasing affluence of the village, for these small stones, bearing no more than the initials and the year of burial, are shaped like an inverted teardrop and demonstrate an increasing desire to mark the passing of loved ones, which had not been affordable until that time. There is no doubt that many more people were buried unmarked or marked by no more than a wooden cross that has rotted away. The presence of the stones coincides with the decision to enlarge the churchyard to the north in 1689, shortly before the north aisle was built onto the church. Lime trees planted in 1760 were removed in 1983 when most were found to be in a dangerous condition.

***This Earthly World,* written by Revd Austin Lester (rector of Peter Tavy 1908–32) during the Easter weekend of 1949, shortly before he died, and sent to Mrs John Vogwill.**

You tell me I am getting old, but that's not really so.
The house I live in may be worn and that of course I know,
It's been in use a good long while and weathered many a gale,
I'm therefore not surprised to find it's getting somewhat frail.

You tell me I am getting old, you mix my house with me,
You're looking at the outside, that's all that most folk see,
The dweller in the little house is young and bright and gay,
Just starting on a life that lasts through long eternal day.

The colour changing of the roof, the windows getting dim,
The walls a bit transparent and getting rather thin,
The foundations not so steady as once they used to be
And that is all that you observe, but it is not really me.

I patch the old house up a bit to make it last the night
But soon I shall be flitting to my home of endless light.
I'm going to live for ever there, my life goes on, it's grand.
How can you say I'm getting old? You do not understand.

These few short years can't make me old, I feel I'm in my youth,
Eternity lies just ahead, full life and joy and truth.
We will not fret to see this house grow shally day by day,
But look ahead to our new home which never will decay.

I want to be made fit to dwell in that blest house above,
Cleansed in the precious blood of Christ and growing still in love.
The beauty of that glorious home, no words can ever say,
'Tis hid from our mortal eyes, but kept for us some day.

My House is getting ready in the land beyond the sky,
Its architect and builder is my Saviour now on high,
But I rather think He's leaving the furnishing to me,
So it's 'treasure up in heaven' I must store each day, you see.

The Clockface

Roger Vere

Jonas Chubb

George Chubb

The engraved stone over the entrance to the old chapel at Shula. Elias Bray was living at the cottage and added this extension to accommodate the Methodists in the village, but they later built a larger chapel, now called Laurel House.

Above: *The Tree of Memories, prepared for the 75th Anniversary of the Methodist chapel in 1955. All the memories of local Methodists who had attended the chapel, as well as the ministers who had served the circuit, were sought and inscribed on the leaves.*

Left: *The chapel during renovations, 1989–92.*

Below: *Outside the chapel, 1979. Left to right, back row: in the doorway, Kathryn Dingle, Florrie Williams, Frank Bellamy; front row: Matthew Wood, Revd R. Pope, Revd L. Smith, Revd I. Earl, Dorothy Maunder, ?, ?, Peter Earl, Ida Lynd, Ivy Cooper, Debbie Ball, Pauline Ball, Mrs R. Dodd, Tracey Watts (girl in front).*

The Methodist Chapel

Although Methodism had started as a revivalist movement within the Church of England as far back as 1730, it was not until the death of John Wesley in 1791 that it actually broke with the established Church. In Peter Tavy, as with much of the West Country, Methodist preachers drew large numbers to their meetings, with a significant number being attracted by the Bible Christian movement within the Methodist fold. It is said that the well-known preacher Billy Bray preached in Peter Tavy around 1830 and as a result Elias Bray was moved to build the small chapel attached to Shula in 1833. However, the main body of Methodists felt they needed a larger building. It was in this frame of mind that what came later to be known as the 'Reading Room', now Laurel House, was built in the following year. It is probable that the Bible Christian members in the village used the chapel at Shula, though by 1851 they had either returned to the Methodist movement or joined the Bible Christians at meetings in Mary Tavy, where the Zoar Chapel had attendances of 80 to 90 at their afternoon and evening services, as well as meetings in the kitchen of a cottage in the village on Sundays once a fortnight. Some villagers say that Bible Christian services were held at the Reading Room when the Methodists moved to their new chapel. However, there is no evidence in Bible Christian records of a chapel at Peter Tavy.

From 1834 the Methodist movement in the village grew steadily. On 30 March 1851, when the Religious Census was taken, 33 had attended the afternoon service and 60 had attended the evening service, comparing well with St Peter's which had 75 at morning service and 97 at the afternoon service. By the middle of the 1870s they were again looking for a larger meeting-place. It was with some pride that they sought a loan from the central committee of the Methodist movement and approached the Duke of Bedford for land on which to build. In March 1879 they submitted an application to build a new chapel, claiming that their number of 'regular hearers' was now 50 and that they wished to build a chapel capable of seating 130 as the present chapel accommodated only 60. Even this must have been a tight fit for the space at the old chapel. The cost was to be £380, of which £280 had already been promised. In June that year the central Wesleyan Committee replied:

The Committee do not think this a case to be aided by loan. They very reluctantly consent to a debt of £70 and hope that an early effort will be made to pay it off.

The Peter Tavy Band of Hope gathered at the Pannier Market, Tavistock for their parade through the streets in support of Temperance (abstinence from alcohol). Jonathan Weeks is standing on the very left of the picture.

Sunday School, Methodists, c.1950. The picture includes: Maurice Greening, Keith Brown, John Pellowe, John Bellamy, Doreen Dingle, Marianne Pellowe, Wendy Greening, Bill Dodd, Bill Bellamy, Barbara Martin, ?, Ruth Bellamy.

Right: *Reg and Molly Cummings were the first people to be married in the chapel at Peter Tavy in 1959. There were no further weddings at the chapel until 1969 when her niece, Brenda, married Dennis Williams.*

The old chapel was converted into a Reading Room for the village at the end of the nineteenth century. Note the rectangular plaque on the wall which was removed when the Reading Room was converted into a house in the 1980s and now lies at the entrance to the new chapel. The building is now called Laurel House.

This was not as severe as it sounded as they went on to make a grant of £30 from their central funds that covered the immediate costs and allowed the debt 'to be paid off by local efforts within ten years'. In a matter of days, John Garland Bray and his son John Henry (Ida Lynd's father), together with George Vogwill had started work on the building. It was deliberately built to allow a balcony to be added when required, but the failure of the mines meant that the population dropped and this was never needed.

By 1900 numbers had fallen and the chapel needed repair so it was decided to hold a campaign for funds to restore it. Edward Dodd was in the forefront of those who, in the following year, invited Mrs Florence Taylor to come to the village to lead a revival at which more than 30 villagers joined the Methodist movement. Funds were duly raised to carry out repairs.

At much the same time Jonathan Weeks, who with his wife Polly ran one of the shops in the village, held Temperance meetings which led to the very active Peter Tavy Band of Hope, known as the Peter Tavy Blues, with more than 50 members. So successful was their crusade by 1916 that when George V announced that he would refuse alcohol until the end of the war, the Parish Council petitioned the Magistrates Court in Tavistock to revoke the liquor licence of the Peter Tavy Inn and shut it down. A wise magistracy deferred a decision and the matter never returned to court for consideration.

In November 1954 members of the chapel held their 75th anniversary. Phyllis Dodd recalls that in the previous year an auction was held when various items, including a pig and chickens, were sold to raise money to re-plaster the walls. During the celebrations a 'Tree of Memories' was prepared and

This significant extension to the cottage, Shula, which can be seen at the far left of the picture, was built in 1833 by Elias Bray and was used for a short time by the Bible Christian movement.

many people related their memories, which were inscribed on leaves, some even recalling the original building of the chapel where two small cottages, that had replaced a mining agent's house, were knocked down to make space. Others told how they looked forward to the Sunday School celebrations in June, when the girls would have new dresses, and to the mission services on a Tuesday with a 'magic lantern' show. These Tuesday meetings for the young people of the village became so popular that a Guild of Youth was formed, later to transfer to the Village Hall as a youth club. Regular concerts, plays, walks and barbeques were held. Molly Cummings recalls that at Christmas time a nativity play was performed and large parties would go out on foot, singing carols as far away as Coxtor and Godsworthy. Frederick William Dodd was especially remembered for the extra-strong mints that he always handed around the party! Then, of course, there was the 'outing'. Bert Cole's bus was called into service to take the party on a trip to Looe, Paignton or Teignmouth.

In 1979 the centenary was celebrated with special services, but it was not long before a closer inspection of the building showed major work was required, so in 1987 the chapel was closed. Services were transferred to the Parish Church and the work of reconstruction began. Work was done to replace the roof and the interior needed to be fully redecorated. Everyone joined in and although there had been something of a divide between the church and chapel, people of all persuasions gave a helping hand. The kitchen and toilet were not added until 1993/94, but Mrs Jessie Bellamy and Mrs Ida Lynd, the oldest serving members, reopened the chapel in 1991.

Shortly after the Gulf War, in which her father had become involved, Anna and David Dodd were married at the chapel. This 'going-away car' was constructed by friends to celebrate the occasion.

A view of the chapel following redecoration in 1992. An entrance has now been provided at the side of the house, out of sight in this picture.

CUDLIPPTOWN, THE HAMLETS & SORTRIDGE

Cudlipptown was not in the parish of Peter Tavy until 1884, when it was transferred from the parish of Tavistock; at the same time the manor of Sortridge broke its connections with Peter Tavy and transferred to Whitchurch.

The manor of Culitone appears in the Domesday Book, although it seems that the name is derived from a Saxon thegn named Cudda, in whose settlement alongside the River Tavy there was a crossing or 'lype'. The manor was granted to the abbey at Tavistock by William the Conqueror, but was illegally transferred by the Abbot to his brother, William, shortly afterwards. An edict was required from Henry I to restore the manor to the abbey in 1120. In 1193 a person named Cudlipp was amongst those whose lands were seized following a failed rebellion against Richard I. Two years later, the Archdeacon family, who owned the manor of Morwell, offered the King ten marks for the manor of Cudlipp and bound the two manors to Tavistock until the separation 700 years later. The ownership of the lordship of the manor is even more convoluted for it passed into the hands of the Russell family, Dukes of Bedford, along with the abbey lands at the Reformation. By the middle of the seventeenth century it was owned by the Rolle family and afterwards the Sawle family. In 1789 Henry Fellowes, High Sheriff of Devon, sold it to Peter Reddicliffe, who in turn sold it in 1808 to Edward Bray, steward to the Duke of Bedford. As a result of marriage and inheritance, the lordship has passed to the owner at the time of writing, Mr John Kempe. Although the Cudlipp family gave the hamlet its name and owned some land there until 1860, it does not appear that they ever held the lordship themselves after the events of 1193.

Below: *The slotted gate allowed a narrow plank or pole to be inserted into the stone gatepost at one end and rested in a cut into the other post with an upright sleeper to hold it in place. Medieval in origin, they were in use well into the seventeenth century.*

This beautiful curved arch is the doorway to the old medieval farmhouse at Edgcombe.

The Manor } The Court Leet with view of Frankpledge of our
of } Sovereign Lady the Queen and the Court Baron
Cudlipptown } of The Revd John Edward Kempe, Clerk,
Lord of the said Manor held at the House
of Mr Henry Reddicliffe within the said Manor on Tuesday
the 20th day of June 1893.
Before

Edward Chilcott   Gentleman   Steward

John Oxenham	Foreman	John Reddicliffe
John Solomon Skinner	The Jury of our Sovereign	Thomas Martin Rogers
William Arthur	Lady the Queen	John Cole Junr
John Arthur	and the Homage	Henry Reddicliffe
Emmanuel Watkins	Here	Walter Reddicliffe
John Cole		William Rowse

who being sworn and charged upon their Oaths touching
articles of the Court Leet as well as the Court Baron
Present and say as follows —

We present all our ancient customs to be good and
laudable and they ought to be continued.

We present that Mr Henry Reddicliffe be Reeve and
Poundkeeper of the Manor

John Oxenham   Foreman

J. S. Skinner   John Reddicliffe

Wm Arthur   Thomas Martin Rogers

John Arthur   John Cole

Emmanuel Watkins   H Reddicliffe

John Cole   W. Reddicliffe

Opposite: *A report of the Court Leet held at Cudlipptown in 1893. Meeting under the chairmanship of the lord of the manor's steward, Edward Chilcott, John Oxenham is sworn as the foreman and all the others are sworn as the jury. They then presented all 'our ancient customs to be good and laudable and they ought to be continued.' Then Henry Reddicliffe was presented as the reeve and pound keeper of the manor. Following this they would sit down to a meal at the expense of the lord of the manor. They would commonly have presented a case that someone outside the manor had allowed his sheep or cattle to pasture on their land and should be fined, or that following the death of a tenant, a successor was approved and wished to pay a fine to the lord of the manor to be allowed to take over the tenancy of the house and land.*

Right: *This damaged but clearly circular whorl was used with a spindle through the hole to spin wool into a thread for weaving. Originating as far back as the Bronze Age, similar ones made entirely of wood are still in use today. The size and weight determine the thickness of the resulting wool thread.*

Below: *A map of Cudlipptown taken from the 1884 Ordnance Survey by George Haine. It shows the three farms, Edgcombe, before the present house was built, Kinsmans which is now derelict and Cudlipptown on the east of the lane through the hamlet. Manor House Farm dominates the land to the west of the map.*

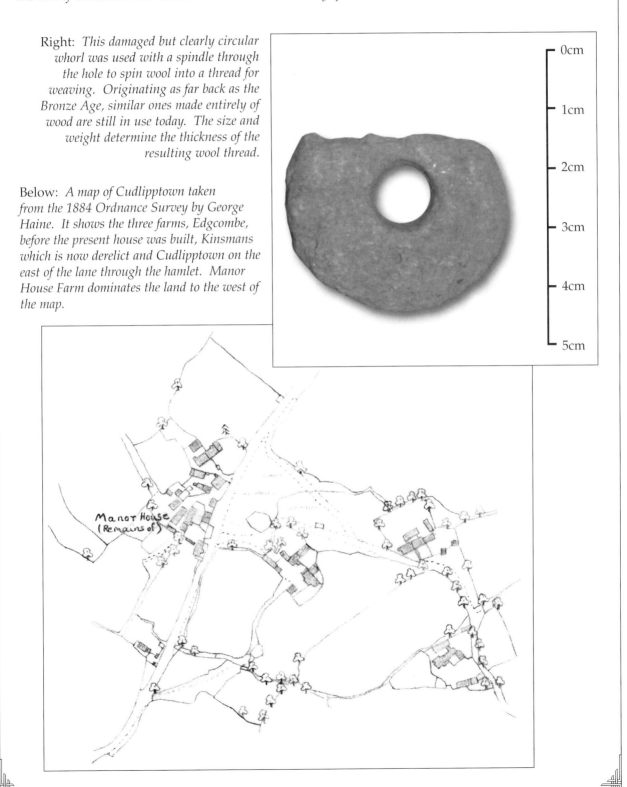

A one-cent coin of the nineteenth century, from the USA, found in Cudlipptown.

A small lead figurine, 42mm high, found at Higher Manor, Cudlipptown.

A plaque (190mm x 130mm) found at Cudlipptown.

A silver groat from the reign of Edward IV (1471–83). Minted in London, it was the last 'front-faced portrait' of a monarch to be used on an English coin. It was found during the restoration of a house at Cudlipptown.

Beating the Bounds at Cudlipptown 1981. Left to right back row; *Peter Cox, John Collins, Peter Tinson, ?, Jennifer Hilborn, Neil Mudge, Stan Mudge;* middle row; *Kathleen Haine, Pearl Tinson, Peter Hilborn, Jack Dawe, Wendy Hilborn, Jessie Cole;* front row: *Pamela Tinson, the other children have not been identified.*

Cudlipptown

Janet Bedford

Cudlipptown is a small hamlet situated a mile north-east of Peter Tavy. The unusual name probably derives from the personal name of a Saxon thegn, Cudda, known to have held lands in this area beside a crossing or 'lype' of the River Tavy. The Saxon word 'lype' is similar to the lowland Scots word 'loup', the language having moved with the people driven northward and westward as the advancing Normans took over the English heartland following the Conquest of 1066. A mounting block in the Scottish borders is called a 'louping-on-stone', indicating its equivalence with today's word 'leap'. Just downstream of the junction of the Cudlipptown Brook, or Burn as it is called locally, is a large, smooth rock that channels the river into a chasm that can be easily leapt at times of normal water levels. Between the eleventh and thirteenth centuries permanent surnames developed from patronymics, so the name Cudlipp was passed on to many families and into general usage. The name can be seen amongst the local tinners and miners in the sixteenth and seventeenth centuries, and from 1505 onwards it is recorded in the names of churchwardens at Tavistock.

The oldest inhabited site within the manor is 'the pound' on the west side of Whit Tor, about 300 feet below the summit. There are six clearly visible hut circles, three of which are against the higher limit with an entrance to the lower north-west border. A little spring ran through the enclosure during the rainy seasons and another stream close by provided a 'modern' convenience for a Bronze-Age community. The enclosures appear to have been occupied for a long period, although Victorian excavations revealed very little evidence of a conclusive nature, apart from a stone scraper.

Reeves provide some evidence of the old boundary, with a track running down to the ancient clapper bridge on Smith Hill from the farm at Twist (Twyste). The bridge is low and double-arched, constructed from surprisingly large stones. On this track, returning to the hamlet, are the old farms of Cudlipptown and Kinsmans. There are very large rocks incorporated into the buildings and hedges all around Cudlipptown, suggesting their ancient origins. Also, near the Green in the centre of the hamlet are the remains of the manor pound, which was used to pen stray animals until the owner reclaimed them after paying his fine to the lord of the manor. The pound was built for Revd Edward Bray in 1842 after he had obtained three separate quotations from local masons. He finally insisted that the stone be taken from Smith Hill and sand for the mortar from Sandy Ford, presumably to keep down the cost. The last standing part was demolished in 1970 as it had become dangerous, but some of the base is still visible. Another bill for the repair of the pound by George Doidge of Harford Bridge is dated 1886. In 1952 the pound was, perhaps surprisingly, listed as an ancient monument.

Two farms are mentioned in the Domesday Book; Twist (Twyste) and the manor. It was a small demesne with land for just two ploughs and two villeins, who held venville rights which, for a small annual payment (5d. per year in 1532), allowed them to pasture sheep and cattle on the moor after sunset. In addition, although no green oak or venison could be taken, they were allowed to take 'all else which would do them good'. This of course included turf and peat for fires and stone for hedging and building. The row of large stones and the pile beside the gate at Twist (Twyste) are said to have been collected at a later date by a couple hoping to build a freeholding on the moor. At that time if you could build a cottage, with the help of your neighbours, and light a fire in a day you could live there permanently. This couple were discovered by the local people and stopped before they could do it.

During the ownership of the manor by Tavistock Abbey it is claimed that monks were sent to Cudlipptown to recuperate after an illness. However, there are no ecclesiastical buildings in the area and it is not known where they stayed. There is still a road called Church Lane, between Cudlipptown and Wapsworthy, which may provide a clue to the location of such a building.

The Old Farmhouse at Edgcombe, now used as a barn, was built in 1532 for one of the Cudlipp family. Kinsmans is probably older and is now quite derelict. Vere Tenements, which was recently renamed Higher Manor, is of late-medieval date. Brook Cottage, at the entry to the hamlet, was built in about 1650. Broadmoor, which has been renamed White Tor Stables, was rebuilt after a fire in the early-twentieth century. The three prominent late-Victorian houses date from the 'golden age' of farming in the early 1880s. The front of Manor Farm was rebuilt at this time with a mind to 'bringing it up to date'. In 1953 it was rescued and partly restored. At the rear is an old chimney, which served a hearth and cloam oven for bread baking, and a rounded corner, suggesting even possible Saxon origins.

A row of cottages has completely disappeared opposite Brook Cottage, although the derelict remains of one can be seen, set back from the road amongst the trees. The field that now stands there has the name 'Stoney', which may indicate that there are remains of a building therein.

The last Manor Court to be held in Cudlipptown was in 1924 and was recalled by James Cole of Moorview in a conversation during 1964. He remembered that, 'A feast after the meeting included a

Below: *Manor Farmhouse, 1957.*

A view of Manor House Farm in 1970. It is suggested that the small house in the foreground was the old farmhouse and that perhaps the bigger house at the back is the old manor house.

round of beef and two bottles of gin.' James went on to describe how there were two solicitors present but the rest were farmers, one of whom had to stay and sleep off his gin before leaving to attend his cattle. James Cole also remembered the farmers coming to Manor Farm to pay their rents – they walked down a path laid with white quartz stones, locally known as 'white acres', and would then go into the house to pay their rents, unlike earlier days when all dealings were held in the open. The stones occur naturally in the area and are used by some households to decorate pathways. Broken china and quartz were also used to make the paths to Merrivale more visible in the mist or winter darkness.

The bounds of the manor are beaten every few years and in 1981, when 48 people walked the boundary, they recorded their route:

... followed a course from a lay-by close to Horndon Lane across Joll's to the river and along the eastern hedge. Climbing from there to the road then thirty yards along the road towards Wapsworthy before entering Wheatlands on our right. Followed the hedge between Wheatlands and Bowhays in a southerly direction to the moorgate. Turning eastwards now on the moor we followed the hedge in an easterly direction to the gate leading to Wapsworthy. Passing the gate we continued easterly along Broadmead hedge to the corner with Butterberries. Turning south we followed Butterberries hedge to the top of Cudlipptown Down where the hedge turns east. We continued to follow the hedge to Lanson Moor, before turning due west on the Military road.

We continued down this road past Stephen's Grave into Twist Lane, stopping for lunch at Twist Barn. From Twist corner we followed a path to Boulters Tor, from there to the great rock on Smerdon Down. From the great rock we took a line to Round Field Corner and then followed the hedge in a northerly direction to Blackshields (sic) Corner on Smerdon Down. Here we climbed over into Mr Rowse's ground and followed the hedge dividing Mr Rowse's and Mr Abel's fields in a northerly direction to the road from Peter Tavy to Cudlipptown. Crossing this we continued north across Little Minefield and along the hedge on the western side and followed the continuation in the mine ground until we met the Tavy.

How accurate this boundary was can be judged from the tales of how villagers from Peter Tavy, on hearing of the intention to beat the bounds of Cudlipptown, would gather on the top of Smear Ridge with stones and clods of earth to drive them away from the great rock on Smeardon Down to the hedge that encloses Bryan Rowse's field. No such battle took place in 1981, or apparently had done for some time!

The precise position of the manor house is not clear, although the back walls of Manor Farm are

Twyste (Twist) Farm, one of the oldest venville holdings, lying in the moor. The tenants had a right, for a small fee, to take what they wanted for their own use from the moor, apart from oak and venison. It is now derelict and returning to the moor.

three feet thick and the garden contains plentiful amounts of pottery shards and other artefacts, such as a clay spindle whorl. Most of these were found in the stone hedges or lying in the bed of a nearby stream. 'Gypsy' Orchard, a traveller who had lived in the area and frequently returned, remembered that the shippen near the lane was the farmhouse and that the manor house was further back. Both buildings were built in around the twelfth century and could be older, at least in part. It is doubtful that the manor house was ever a large mansion because, to quote J.M. Synge, 'in this wild and windy corner of the distant hills' with a land area no more than 1,100 acres, excluding the forest grazing, great wealth would not have been possible. This was a small manor that was little affected by agricultural changes from Saxon times to the mid-nineteenth century. Veare Tenements has a number of medieval features and a silver groat was found there when the old privy was cleared.

Land was sold off gradually until just seven working farms remained by 1900, which had dwindled to four by 1960; at the time of writing in 2002 just two remain. The fields are widely distributed amongst the farms as a result, so it is said, of card games where fields served to cover the players' losses. A number of gateposts still have their medieval slots for poles that were held in position by sleepers and wedges. More recently the author John Arden lived in Manor Farm Cottage and wrote the much-enacted *Sergeant Musgrave's Dance* whilst sitting in the garden during the early years of 1950. The play is still performed and until recently was part of the school curriculum for English literature.

In 1832, as the Reform Bills were working their way through Parliament, an issue arose over the right of the tenants at Cudlipptown to a parliamentary electoral vote. Cudlipptown was still part of the ecclesiastical parish of Tavistock and it seems that the Bill was so drafted that when it was passed Cudlipptown tenants lost their right to vote. A parliamentary debate followed the discovery and the matter was put right a few months later. Mrs Bray, whose husband Revd Edward Atkyns Bray was a lord of the manor, comments at length in one of her books about the fact that he was not informed of the matter, otherwise it would not have happened. It was not until 1884 that the ecclesiastical parish was separated from Tavistock and became part of the parish of Peter Tavy.

American coins found at Cudlipptown may indicate a migration of miners from the area to America, or indeed people from the area may have been visiting there as early tourists, but they are not the oldest coins to be found there. The silver groat found at Vere Tenements dates to Edward IV's reign of 1473–83.

Until the 1950s wood and turf were the most common domestic fuels, and trees were cut down or pollarded to provide the wood. The change of fuels to oil and gas resulted in the landscape altering, with trees growing to full stature creating more woodlands. In 1940 a farmer's wife could hoist a small flag at the house to signal when dinner was ready and the farmer could see it from most of his fields. This would now be impossible. The pollard bole of a large ash can still be seen at the side of the road as one enters the hamlet.

The use of water power was not neglected and a small water-wheel on Cudlipptown Brook was, until recent years, connected by a long steel rod to machinery in the nearby farm. Here it powered a circular saw for cutting logs and in season was connected to the threshing machine.

This small clapper bridge crosses the Cudlipptown Brook on the path to Smith Hill. It is clearly very old and the rocks and two arches have stayed in place through many floods.

As yet unexplained is the circular enclosure in the centre of Cudlipptown Green. On old maps it is referred to as the Duke of Bedford's land, although he had given up the manor many years previously. Some of the stones at the base of the encircling hedge are incredibly large, suggesting that they even possibly formed there. The hedge certainly appears to be of a great age and, although rather large, it could be the Norman pound which is believed to have existed in the manor. At the time of writing it is planted as an orchard and is private land in the ownership of Peter Tinson of Edgcombe Farm.

Devon United Mines 1906 Ltd.

The Central Mine was sited some 250 yards west of the Cudlipptown Brook. A leat from the River Tavy served both this mine and the south mine with water power. A tramline ran down river connecting the two mines and carrying ore for treatment at the lower mine. A shaft was sunk to about 200 feet and ran due east under the fields for some 300 yards.

The South Mine lay close upriver from the Mary Tavy Clam and had much more extensive workings. In 1909 an adit south-west of the Clam ran under the fields for some 300 feet but the larger part of the mine was served by a shaft about a quarter of a mile further upriver which had been sunk to some 150 feet deep, with level tunnels extending under fields to the west of Cudlipptown Lane.

Both mines had closed down by the end of the First World War.

Above: *White Acres, the path to Manor House Cottage taken by generations of tenants when paying their quarterly rents. The path was so named because of the white quartz paving.*

Below: *The site of the old manor pound, built in 1842 for the Revd Bray who was lord of the manor at that time. Some of the original wall can be seen forming a corner to the right of the picture.*

Peter Tavy Hamlets

The Peter Tavy hamlets were a group of widely dispersed farming settlements to the north of the village and west of the River Tavy. The largest, and perhaps most important of them, is the old manor of Willsworthy, referred to in Domesday as Wifleurde, held by Alfred the Breton, and owned by Siward before the Conquest. There was land for four ploughs (only one was held for the lord of the manor) with 12 acres of woodland and pasture some two leagues long by one wide. The whole area included in the hamlets took in the farms at Beardon (also an ancient enclosure), Barewalls, Reddaford, Hilltown, Standon, Yellowmead, Old Mead, Lanehead, Gnattor and Will. Most are old mining areas that were enclosed as farms, but no doubt they benefited from both activities. From medieval times there was a steady turnover of tenants and owners until the mining fever had abated. The manor of Willsworthy was in the overall ownership of the Tremayne and Calmady Hamlyn families for many years, but the Buller family, who owned land to the west including much in Mary Tavy, bought it from them. It is not clear quite when this occurred but could have been at the time Edward Bray purchased and enclosed land around Beardon in the early 1800s. The original manor house at Willsworthy has not been identified but the present house at Higher Willsworthy contains many medieval features with the prime possibility

The James Cole family at Cudlipptown. Left to right, back row: Fanny, William, James Henry, Susan (wife of James Henry); front row: James Cole and Tamsin (née Phillips) with James Henry junr (Jim) on her lap, who later married Jessie Bellamy. Susan Cole was the schoolmistress at Peter Tavy School. James Cole went to South Africa and when he returned he built Burnshall and possibly Moorview. It is said that Burnshall was so named as it was intended for a member of the Burn family who was about to marry, but the wedding fell through.

that, like other farmhouses of small estates, the manor house became the farmhouse or *vice versa*, as owners changed or money became more available.

Perhaps Willsworthy is best known for its position on the Lych Way. Before the Bishop gave a dispensation in 1260, all burials had to be carried out at the Parish Church. Lydford Church was the Parish Church for the whole of the forest of Dartmoor and the dead had to be carried from as far away as Babeny on the eastern extreme, a distance of 11 miles as the crow flies. Even those much nearer had a considerable problem, especially in winter, and many tales are still told of how bodies were kept until the weather was more clement, even as late as the last century! The Lych Way at the western end of the village is still discernible as it makes its way over the River Walkham and across Lanson Moor, keeping north of Whit Tor to drop down to Brousentor and the Tavy, then up alongside the farmhouse at Willsworthy (in the occupation of Baldwin de Insula in 1267), before reaching Yellowmead Farm and out on to Blackdown.

The names of those who held the farms in the nineteenth century, and in some instances many years before, are still recalled by villagers. Reep at Hilltown and Gnattor, Rice at Standon, Lanehead and Hilltown, Harvie at Hilltown and Will, and Cole at Willsworthy are still remembered for their hardiness and expert knowledge of the animals they cared for. The Cole family had arrived in Willsworthy around 1670, perhaps taking over when the Kinsman family moved to Cudlipptown.

It is fortunate that soon after the turn of the last century Eliza Harvie, who was living at Hilltown and was supplementing her farming income with paying guests, kept a guest book from which the following quotations are taken:

5 July 1909.
I have fished the Tavy from Horndon Clam to its source... In dry weather when the river is low... two to three dozen fish may be taken in a day. My heaviest fish was just under 3lbs and twenty one inches long...
                                    Patrick Stewart.

24 August 1912.
The weather is ruled by the moon, so they say
And we find that the saying is true,
For at Hilltown it rains when the moon's at the full,
And it rains when the moon's at the new.
When the moon's at the quarter, then down comes
    the rain.
At the half it's no better, I ween,
When it's at the threequarters, it's at it again.
And mostly it rains in between.
                          Emmeline Corner, Paignton.

26 August 1914.
Dry fly fishers go to Tavy Cleave above the leat, for trout

for breakfast fish Will's Brook with worm, Baggator Brook with worm or Wapsworthy Brook with worm and good water will yield dozens.
Rabbits to be got early morning and about six in the evening.
                                    F. Warner Jones.

5 August 1915.
Thanks to the discovery of a sprig of white heather on the evening of our arrival, we have avoided colds and chills, bulls and bogs, with great success. Fortified by Mrs Harvie's excellent chicken and cream we have courageously faced all four.
                          Mary King and Phöebe Paul.

9 August 1916.
This is the time for Whortleberries in full perfection of which delicious fruit I do not notice much, if any mention.
                R. Gibbings, London and I. Wallers, Plymouth.

July 1909.
My only regret is that I did not carry out to the full my intention of bathing every morning at dawn in the Tavy!!
                                    Patrick Shaw Stewart.

John Arthur, who lived at Cudlipptown, was one of two men from unrelated families with the same name. He was nicknamed 'Little' John, and his namesake 'Big' John.

Manor of Sortridge

The manor of Sortridge is geographically much nearer to Whitchurch than Peter Tavy. However, for reasons not yet discovered, from certainly prior to the seventeenth century, it was an attached part of the parish of Peter Tavy until 1884, when it was separated. The manor was part of the estates of the Glanville family in the seventeenth century and may have been broken up on the death of Francis Glanville, who had six daughters. It passed into the hands of John Pengelly, whose family held it for over 150 years. By marriage it then passed to the Spry family, with whom it remained until the separation from Peter Tavy. Apart from the proper payment of rates, there cannot have been much contact between the manors, although the name Pengelly turns up from time to time when money was being sought for some 'good cause'.

None of the Spry family and only two members of the Pengelly family were buried at Peter Tavy in the 250 years they lived in the area. An alms dish amongst the church silverware, dated 1738 and donated by Henry Pengelly, seems to be the only solid connection. No doubt the parish felt they benefited from the rates collected from the mines of the Sortridge Consols, situated between Whitchurch and Horrabridge in the middle years of the nineteenth century, for a protest was raised by the Parish Council when the separation was first suggested in 1857. The Parish Council complained that they would be penniless and that the rates would be 'prohibitive' if such a decision was made. By 1884 the Sortridge mines had ceased work and the Parish Council made no protests about losing the manor.

The present house at Higher Willsworthy has many medieval features, but may not be the original building due to many 'upgradings'.

Will Farm at Willsworthy, now a centre for horse riding.

Below: *Kathy Crantz came to Peter Tavy from Germany as a student. Many of her sketches decorate* The Peter Tavy Journal. *A consummate artist, she was honoured when the Royal Academy accepted a piece of her work for exhibition.*

Right: *Bryan Rowse was born in Cudlipptown where his parents and grandparents had been farmers for over 100 years. He was Chairman of the Parish Council for many years, and continues to farm from his home that retains the name of the hamlet of Cudlipptown.*

PETER TAVY PUBLICATIONS

The Peter Tavy Journal

Villages change – they grow or maybe dwindle. People leave, die, change their jobs, get married – children are born, houses built, maybe some are demolished. And the countryside and its wildlife change with the seasons and perhaps because of different ways of farming. Lots of small things happen in a typical year – parish councillors attempt to beat the newly changed bounds and fall in the ditches – the village is invaded by the Women's Institute on a treasure hunt, a badger is found in a local henhouse, and a hamster runs amok in the village shop. Bigger issues crop up, the poll tax, proposed legislation on the sale of unpasteurised milk, the Ministry of Defence want to build a new barracks on nearby moorland. Who will remember all the details in the years to come? Villagers in Peter Tavy decided to record everything – or nearly everything – that happened in the community from March 1989 to March 1990.

So wrote Angela Larcombe on the opening page of *The Journal*.

Stored away in the village archives are drawings especially made for the *Journal* by Kathy Crantz and photographs and accounts in great detail, but *The Journal* is an abridged account taken season by season through the year. Here are some extracts:

Spring

A very wet month of March after a very dry January. March 8th brought snow and sleet which turned to heavy rain by 10am. By the afternoon the River Tavy, second fastest flowing river in England, was in full spate and reaching perilously near to the top of the banks. By the end of the month spring had arrived, with daffodils, primroses and lambs. Farmers, who lamb much later here on Dartmoor than their colleagues on kinder land, report that it is going well. In keeping with such things, Sandra Dodd's first baby has arrived, and William is sleeping peacefully in his pram.

Peter and Julie Bellamy are delighted with their new calf. Julie's Christmas present was an embryo Belgian Blue calf which was implanted in one of the Friesian cows. The cow gave birth and a beautiful white heifer is now the nucleus of Julie and Peter's hopes for a new pedigree herd.

The first residential home for the elderly, Spring House, celebrated its first anniversary.

Flowers and birdsong are recorded, but with a wry twist:

NOT ALL the merry whistling comes from the birds. The builders working on the barn conversion at Gatehouse Farm are a cheerful lot. The house is nearly completed and the old farmhouse is up for sale. James Perkins remembers having his tonsils removed in the parlour – quite an original selling point!!

The government plan to stop the sale of unpasteurised milk has united the village in support of local farmer Bill Dodd whose family have supplied milk to the village for three generations. Bill cannot put in pasteurising equipment for so small a quantity of milk and would have to sell his herd of South Devons if the ban goes ahead.

Florrie Williams, who lived alone in the village, fell and hurt her right eye, and as she has no sight in the left eye she spent some time in hospital before coming back to stay at Spring House. She is 88 years old and too frail to return home so the new residential home in the village means she can stay in familiar surroundings and be visited by friends.

The Village is coasting into summer with lots to look forward to. The Youth Club holiday in the Lake District, the Sunday School outing, the filling of the Coombe Pool and of course the Village Fête, with a host of other events that are planned by the new Village Hall Committee.

Peter Tavy's oldest resident Mrs Ida Lynd, born Ida Margery Bray on 9 December 1900 at Gatehouse Farm, moved to Yelverton with her family but returned to Wisdom in 1933. She and her husband had a milk round and small farm which she continued to run after his death in 1962. She played the organ in the Chapel for forty years. [Ida Lynd died in 1996]

Another lady who devoted her life to the village is Jessie Cole who retired this month after being Churchwarden for thirty eight years. She was presented with a specially embroidered kneeler and after a service of favourite hymns a buffet supper was held in the Village Hall.

Gary Metters and Neil Mudge carried off first and second prizes in the Mary Tavy Clay pigeon shoot on Bank Holiday Monday.

Shirley Gill and Sylvia Sankey reported on the local flora and fauna:

An Orange tip butterfly has been seen probably because Lady Smock is flowering well this year. Yellow Brimstones are also around with day flying moths. A Burnet had been identified. Goldfinch, longtailed tits and greenfinches are in the village and surrounding hedgerow.'

Thirteen youngsters went off to the Lake District, led by David Dodd. Many memories, particularly of the climb to the top of Helvellyn at 3118 feet, and the anxious fifty yard sprint required from their camp site to the toilets!

Summer

The Village sweltered through June with no rain falling until the very end. Anxious gardeners were out every evening with watering cans and hosepipes – until the water authority imposed a ban on June 24. Bees droned in the hedges and babies grizzled fretfully in the hot

afternoons. In school unfortunate teenagers wrestled with important exam papers. Peter Tavy's many watercourses seemed cool and inviting as the tar melted on the roads. But stream and river levels were low and even the water flowed slowly in the village. Sheep gratefully gave up their woolly coats to sweating shearers. One thoughtful farmer sheared his sheep dogs along with his sheep – quite mortifying the conventional border collies who slunk off in embarrassment.

It was the parish council annual meeting this month and Bryan Rowse was elected Chairman with Ken Ball his deputy. Formalities over feelings waxed high. The council's opinion of the National Park planners reached an all time low.

Peter Tavy artist Kathy Cranz had an etching of her little daughter accepted for hanging in the Royal Academy Summer Exhibition. (Kathy has drawn the illustrations for The Journal).

Survey forms asking what the village wanted from the Village Hall were distributed. Three hundred were sent out and ninety eight returned. An overwhelming number said the present hall should be retained and more than the essential refurbishment required by the entertainments licence officer should be done.

A barbecue marked the filling of the Coombe pool, some sunbathed others enjoyed hotdogs and watched the dragonflies.

Visitors leaving the post office are intrigued by what appears to be a badly wrapped parcel in the opposite garden. Peter Barnes explains: 'It is a Burrell double crank compound engine of nominal six horse power built in 1916. I am restoring it!'

The local mystery of the Village Cross was raised again. Sightings of possible stones were reported in different parts of the village. It had been taken down from immediately outside the churchyard gate as it stood in the way of turning hearses. Should it be restored? [As a project for the millennium it was restored and now stands close to its original site.]

Bill's second best tractor went up in a blaze of glory in July. It brought the Tavistock firemen dashing through the village to, appropriately enough, Pump Field where the tractor sitting quietly on its own had decided to catch fire. The grass around it and part of the hedge flared up but the firemen quickly had it under control.

Water or rather the lack of it has been uppermost in people's minds. It is certainly becoming a serious matter and Frank Collins is filling milk churns with water to take up to his stock. Edward Dodd has put in a temporary pipe to bring water to a tank on Smeardon Down. Coxtor Well is now dangerously low.

A couple of local successes this month, Peter Tavy Inn won the Tavistock Carnival tug of war, for the second year running, and Sylvia Sankey found a dog for Mrs Lynd. May Wakeham had a sheepdog that was unable to work as the other dogs kept attacking it. Fortunately it had taken to Mrs Lynd and was now her shadow.

The warm dry weather is a mixed blessing. The high moor farmers are having to take water up to Smeardon, but the centre of the moor is still moist. Sheep and cattle are being tempted by succulent grasses growing in the raised bogs. A few foolhardy sheep are venturing onto dangerous sections of the moor. Cattle being heavier are at even greater risk and several farmers have had to rescue cows stuck up to their necks in the treacherous bogs.

A fitting end to the month came with the village 'It's a Knockout' competition. Four teams with the unlikely names of the Lettuce Leaves, Peter Tavy Teapots, Peter Tavy Posse and The Donkeys, bravely took to the field not knowing what was in store. All the games were inevitably accompanied by lots of water, and just as the last, and wettest game started, it began to rain. The Donkeys won, but the judges were of course booed and accused of shortsightedness!

August has seen an abundance of mushrooms this year, but very little grass. The price of hay now above £120 a ton. The price of an average lamb has dropped to about £27 a head, over £6 less than last year. Summer dipping is no longer compulsory as sheep scab has been virtually eradicated.

You could learn a lot at a Village Fayre, how to tie a fly for instance, how to cope with bees, shear a sheep, thatch a roof, spin a skein of wool, tack up a pony and trap, identify minerals and even get a picture on canvass. You could buy pretty well anything from homemade jam and cake to a 1974 AA handbook or a wind up dolphin or buddleia cutting. The energetic could play skittles for a china pig, fight it out on a slippery pole, ride a donkey or go off on a treasure hunt. Those who felt like trying their luck could buy raffle tickets, try the tombola or a lucky dip and even guess how much milk Gran the cow would yield when milked at 4 o'clock. And always a popular event you could buy a plastic duck to win the race down the Colley Brook to Lower Mill.

A country tradition came under scrutiny when Susan Phillpotts recounted the history of the local Hunt:

The Spooners and West Dartmoor Hunt has been in existence since before the turn of the century (1900) yet the whole of their hunting country is on loan from the adjoining packs of the Lamerton and Dartmoor Hunts. For the last five years Spooners has been a committee run hunt with Tim Millar the acting Master for the three seasons and Adrian Dangar the acting Master and huntsman for two seasons. They continue in a line of Masters and huntsmen that started with Colonel Arthur Kelly who hunted a pack of harriers between 1770 and 1823. It was Clarence Spooner, a Plymouth draper who bought the hounds in 1911 and called them 'Mr Spooner's Harriers', and the Spooners title has remained with the pack to this day. The pack starts its traditional season on the first Saturday in November though the hounds will have been out cub hunting since mid-August. During the season they meet on Tuesdays and Saturdays, and expect to kill some 90 foxes.

Autumn
September brought the standpipes. Not just like that of course. Various officials plodded round the village with clipboards and important expressions. Then men in overalls came and peered down hydrants. Then more men in overalls appeared carrying cans of blue paint and the village came out in a nasty rash of blue blobs, blobs just meant hydrants, blue SPs denoted where standpipes were to go. One in Langsford Road, one outside Genesta, one outside the old post office and one down by the pub. The standpipes themselves arrived on September 9 and were put up – but without taps! On September 11 and 12 we had heavy rain and thunderstorms, after a couple of dull days more heavy rain and South West Water announced a reprieve from the planned use of standpipes. It was all put off for a week. The standpipes stayed up for a while, mute and impotent, then they were all taken away. The blue blobs will remain for a long time to come.

With impeccable timing:

The Village Hall Working Party bent on getting urgent waterproofing done before winter met on the dot of 8.30 in the morning of September 10 to deal with the toilet roof. Geoff Porter arrived, his car loaded with tools. John Douglas, Alison and Derek Skillicorn started waterproofing the kitchen wall. John Varnai and John Phillpotts started at roof level with the guttering and moved on to slates. Bryan Rowse began rubbing down and priming the windows, also replacing lost putty. Mary Phillpotts and Angela Collins came forward with coffee and biscuits, and went on to cook beefburgers and onions for lunch with endless cups of tea to follow.

Local young farmers won the tug of war at Modbury to become the South Devon Champions. With more train-

ing they reckon to go further next year.

Lots of small copper butterflies, ladybirds and bees to be seen. A charm of fourteen goldfinch played in Lucy Park, BUT there are millions of flies. The hedges have been cut back, and the fern is turning brown. The annual visit of the road sweeper passed through in the month.

Vi and Alf Burden, both aged 76, had their Golden Wedding anniversary on 30 September. They first met in 1934, Vi was nursing at the West Middlesex Hospital and Alf managed to find a job there and was promptly told off for having a torn coat. 'If you were anything of a nurse you would mend it for me' he said. She did, he asked her to the cinema and so began their long life together.

Sylvia Sankey has been keeping a close eye on her ducks and making sure that they are securely locked up at night because local badgers are now coming down as far as Frank Collins' orchard.

September marks the end of summer, bonfires are lit as folk clear their gardens, soon the regular procession of cows through the village will come to an end as the beasts are wintered in doors.

James Perkins was seen hurrying through the village with a large unbaked apple pie, so large that Mrs Perkins had found at the crucial moment that it would not go into her oven. It was destined for the Church Harvest Festival so an urgent phone call went out. Shirley Gill measured her Rayburn oven and found it would just fit. A hasty transfer worked out well for the sixty or so people who attend the Harvest Supper after the Service. £264 was collected for the Royal Commonwealth Society for the Blind.

The Fatstock Market at Tavistock is the scene for the annual Dartmoor pony sale:

The produce sold is from the pony drift when local owners of mares get together and clear the moors. The ponies from Peter Tavy Common, Langstone Moor, Cox Tor, Roos and Staple Tor are drifted to Moortown to be sorted. Meanwhile ponies on the muster side of the Walkham are drifted towards Merrivale. This tradition is gradually dying out because of public opinion and pressure to stop the sale of horse meat. This has depressed outlets and demand has fallen, prices tumbled and with them the number of ponies. One farmer involved said that in the last nine years the price of ponies was less now than then and the

numbers of mares had halved. Prices this year for a good colt were between £15–£20. [Ponies in 2000 were being offered at 50p each.]

Another market held in October was the 63 Annual Scotch Blackface sheep. The sale is unique to the area as the particular breed is locally popular and grazes in rough conditions on Dartmoor. The Roskillys of Nutley swept the board with prizes.

Edward Dodd professed traditional weather law: If the old saying be true, 'Ice in November to hold up a duck, the rest of the winter will be slush and muck.'

This year many farmers are checking and double checking their sheep. Most are reporting that too many sheep are unaccounted for. As Richard Abel has always said. 'Dartmoor will always have its rent.' Some are bound to fall prey to the elements and the wildlife, but this year it looks as if someone else is having a rent as well, namely rustlers.

The Church bells are still silent, repairs are awaiting a visit from the diocesan expert to determine what needs to be done to make them safe. Neighbouring Whitchurch held a folk dance and donated half the proceeds specifically to the St Peter's Bell restoration fund.

Winter

Christmas in the village started on 1 December with the Chapel Christmas tree – an old tradition which has died out in most other chapels but is kept alive in Peter Tavy. The Chapel was full, each member bought a numbered ticket and after entertainment by a talented family from Cornwall the Christmas tree was stripped of the numbered gifts matching the tickets. A pleasant evening ended with supper.

Mrs Ida Lynd and Mr Bill Bellamy were 89 this month and Tracey Jeffery celebrated her 18th birthday.

The carol singers were out again visiting every house in the parish, even the far flung outposts on the moor. Rain and gales held things up a bit but gradually the singers worked their way round the village, up to Cudlipptown and onwards to Wapsworthy and Willsworthy. Then back on the last evening to Mrs Lynd's on 23 December to open the tins and count the money. £173 was raised half of which was donated to Ethiopian famine relief.

Heavy rain 20 December with thunder and lightning brought the 'dump' water running in the village. Water seeping up from holes between flagstones and in the middle of metalled roads is so named. Many years ago it was believed that the water came from a large pond at the back of the village dump on Smeardon. However, the pond has long since been filled in but water behaving in this way in the village is still called 'dump' water.

The Village Hall heating has been playing up but in spite of it the Parish Council muffled with anoraks and blowing through their fingers plodded bravely through their agenda. Miss Ann Cole was appointed Clerk and was warmly welcomed.

During the next month or two the trout and salmon will be making their way up the rivers. Brown and rainbow trout live their entire lives in our waters, some growing to a respectable size. Looking over the bridge in the village you often see trout six inches or more in length. During the fishing season much bigger trout than these can be caught in the Tavy. Salmon have been spawning in the Colley Brook and head waters of the Tavy for many thousands of years. Poaching is an age old skill still being practised, so water bailiff Robin Armstrong is kept busy patrolling the parish river banks. One other 'poacher' is the Heron who patrols the Colley Brook and can consume a great deal of fish in a day.

January was dominated by hurricane force winds. Hardly anyone escaped damage to property of one sort or another. A hair raising accident at Cudlipptown occurred when Bryan Rowse and Elon Ellicott were trying to clear a large sycamore from the road. Elon's chainsaw was much the largest and others stepped back after taking off some of the side branches, to let him deal with the trunk. Elon sat astride the trunk and was cutting away when all of a sudden the remaining stump of the tree stood upright and from the road the onlookers saw Elon and about half ton of wood being catapulted through the air. He landed some 15 to 20 feet down the field with the wood sailing on another four or five feet. Elon was a little shocked but soon recovered, seeing the funny side of it he took it out on the remaining stump cutting it down to ground level.

A large metal sheet has covered a hole in the road outside the Village Hall. A culvert is being investigated and Peter Barnes, who knows about these things, explained. It was probably constructed 150 years ago by prisoners from Dartmoor who carried out vast amounts of building work locally, most of it was walls but also stone culverts and roads. This particular drain is made of cut sections of granite probably from Merrivale. The culvert had been causing flooding across the road and the blockage was found to be a cover stone that had broken. It has been replaced by a manhole to enable easier cleaning.

Swiss army knives, secateurs and strong gloves have become a necessity for walking in the Coombe. The sheep there seem to have an uncanny knack of getting themselves caught in brambles and have to be cut free. Giving as you approach every appearance of total exhaustion they then deliver their rescuer a swift kick on the shins before diving headlong into the next thicket and getting caught up again.

A recollection of Edward Dodd's should provoke some thought:

In the past 20 years I can remember farms in the village that have fallen 'prey to progress'. Lower and Higher Churchtown, Youlditch, Higher Wapsworthy, Row Farm, Moor View, Gatehouse, Langsford and Lower Collaton have all ceased working as farms. The sad thing is that all these farms once provided a living for a family and the loss of such families has changed the face of rural life. Most of the people who live in these farmhouses do not feel it necessary to understand rural life and the way things work in the country. They don't earn their living from it, they only live there.

February 27 1990 goes down in history. It was Shrove Tuesday, and the weather chucked everything at Peter Tavy. In the course of 24 hours there was wind, rain, sleet, snow, hail, thunder, lightning and even a patch of sunlight.

The shortage of forage made last summer is now reflected in the availability and price of hay. Fetching £115 a tonne for good meadow hay. The milder weather has enabled farmers to reduce rations for outwintered cattle as the grass has been stimulated into growth.

And so the year of recording comes to an end. One villager working for a degree surveyed how long residents had lived in the village. About half had been here more than 20 years and most of the remainder five years or less. He calculated that in another 20 years Peter Tavy will be a ghost village with everyone working elsewhere.

The Peter Tavy Piper

The *Piper* first appeared in May 1984. Although attempts had been made in the 1970s to start a village news sheet, on this occasion grants from the Community Council of Devon and the Peter Tavy Parish Council provided money for an intended run of regular editions every two months for a year. Advertising space was also sold to help cover the expense. The *Piper* was to be available free to every household in the parish, but delivery depended upon a network of volunteers. People living in the centre of the village were encouraged to pick up their copy from the Post Office at Jasmine Cottage or from the Mobile Library on its fortnightly visit to the Square.

The first edition, as indeed almost every edition since, recorded the need for refurbishment of the Village Hall. On this occasion it was the small back room that was soon to be undertaken by unemployed teenagers through the 'Pathfinder Scheme'. The foundation of the 'Minnows' mother-and-baby group in 1982 is mentioned together with their move from the chapel to the Village Hall. A Leisure Group had also been formed under the chairmanship of John Douglas, with Barbara Butterfield as Secretary and Pat Porter as Treasurer. They were to oversee the improvements to the children's playing-field, the pool in the Coombe and the launch of the *Piper*.

It was reported in the first edition that a new parish notice-board had been erected, but the formal opening was interrupted when the protective glass in the door frame fell out on the Parish Clerk!

Notice was given of the proposal to 'beat the bounds' on 26 May with a ban on children under eight years. The 'bounds' were to be restricted to 'the northern section covering Willsworthy, Beardown, Tavy Cleave and Wapsworthy.' The distance was thought to be about 15 miles, and a picnic would be held at half way.

A number of recipes and food tips were printed with a 'Cookery Quiz' followed by a section on gardening which included a formula for compost for pot plants.

A Peter Tavy Archive, between 16–20 June, was also announced, to be held at Harewood House. Michael Guest, who put the archive together, reported that he already had some old Rate Books, William Box's mathematics book and papers showing the cost of setting up house in nineteenth-century Devon. Some of the Rate Books and the Parish Registers are now held at the Devon Record Office but William Box's book and other papers have not been traced. The Heritage Group would be delighted to find them again.

Perhaps the saddest comment is in the advertisement on the back page which refers to the Village Shop and Post Office that sold 'fresh fruit and vegetables, groceries, cigarettes, sweets, ices, frozen food, coal, paraffin, toys, gifts and offered home delivery.' There was a Tea Garden run by Chris and Ann Pollard alongside the shop.

Production of the *Piper* was in the hands of a committee made up of:

Barbara BUTTERFIELD	*Bargain Ads. and Diary*	*The Old Post House, who first drew the logo, used ever since.*
Annette CUDMORE	*Reporter*	*1, Mill Cottages*
John & Judy DOUGLAS	*Production*	*Midhurst Cottage*
Mary FRIEND	*Reporter*	*1, Village Way*
Michael GUEST	*Advertising*	*Harewood*
Pat PORTER	*Treasurer and Reporter*	*Tanglin*
Linda READ	*Production*	*Weir Cottage*
Julie DeQUICK	*joined the team at the end of the first year.*	

In the second edition, two months later, it is clear that the invitation to contribute had been taken up by some villagers. A short article by David Mudge on the 'Farmer's View' and why they complain so much (!) and more on food. A joke space seems to have crept in with a contribution from Sally-Ann Gill. 'How do you know that Moses wore a wig?' 'Because sometimes he was seen with Aaron and sometimes without.' Angela Larcombe was already a contributor, on this occasion with a poem about tarring the road through the village.

The two monthly editions seem to have continued in this vein until 1988 when, conscious of the cost, the *Piper* committee decided to print the May edition on foolscap paper instead of the folded book format that had previously been used. It was not a success. There was generally less content and minimal advertising. There were complaints but few seemed willing to take on the production. The publication lapsed. In the spring of 1989 a new edition, again on foolscap, was produced but this time it came back to stay – not in foolscap – but back again to book format and with quarterly instead of two-monthly editions. Those responsible are not recorded.

The committee that started and ran the *Piper* from birth handed over to Alan and Sylvia Sankey who were running the shop. When they retired at Christmas 1996, Steve and Alison Carreck who continue to gather, edit and publish the *Piper* for the parish took up the mantle.

The map from the first Ordnance Survey of 1809, undertaken by Lt Col Mudge, has several interesting features. The road from Tavistock on the east of the Tavy is seen reaching Peter Tavy Cross. Turning left at this point to follow Batteridge Hill down to Harford Bridge, the road continues alongside Harford Farm running below and parallel to the north-south road from Tavistock to Mary Tavy to meet a turning off the old Exeter road at Edamead, which seems to have disappeared completely. Turning right at this junction leads one to a lane running down to the river and crossing, presumably by ford, to the bottom of Shula Lane and so up through Undertown to the village. Oody lane is also shown, with access to Lanxford (Langsford) apparently from Back Lane on its way to Harragrove. Down Lane on its way to the moor shows the turning to Lower Godsworthy above Sharpy Tor down Watery Lane. The road to Cudlipptown and beyond appears to run directly through the houses, with the majority on the west side and a turning towards the river short of the hamlet leading down to one of the mines.

A VILLAGE MISCELLANAE

Maundy Money

Florence Minnie Williams who lived at Fern Cottage died in 1990 at the age of 88 years. Florrie Williams was involved in everything that went on in the village – the WI, the church, the Village Hall. She was a busy and interesting person. The whole village was delighted when she was selected to receive Maundy Money from the Queen at Exeter Cathedral in 1983 as one of the deserving elderly in the West Country.

The Royal Maunds is distributed by the Queen in person to the number of deserving elderly that correspond to her age. The tradition has been held on Maundy Thursday since at least the reign of Elizabeth I (1558–1603) when fish, bread and wine were given. Since 1837, the coins in the form of silver pennies, twopennies, threepences and fourpences have been specially struck for the occasion and have not been changed to conform to decimalisation.

Getting up Steam

'The Pride of the West', a steam engine built in 1916 which was brought to Peter Tavy by Peter Barnes so that it could be restored. Here Peter and son Daryl are seen getting up steam for a trial run in 1989.

Jubilee 1977 or is it 2002? The parish has shown no great concern to change the way it celebrates national events. In 1937 an arch decorated the school entrance with a central crown just as in 2002. In 1898 sports events were enjoyed as in 1977 and 2002. The millennium came in for similar treatment. Sports during the day were followed by food and a dance or entertainment in the evening. This Jubilee a massive beacon was lit on Smear Ridge in company with those on neighbouring peaks.

Radcliffe' Tenants Dinner. Although the Radcliffe (Radclyffe) family had been owners of a great many farms and other land in the parish from late in the seventeenth century, between 1880 and 1950 nearly all of it was sold, often to the current tenant. In the periods before and after the First World War an annual dinner was held for the tenants, usually at the Bedford Hotel in Tavistock. This photograph was taken towards the end of the 1920s.

Left: *Peter Tavy Heritage Group display, Jubilee 2002.*

Right: *Jubilee decorations on the Village Bridge. With Gatehouse Farm in the background the bunting and flags stretched the length and breadth of the village guiding everyone to the sports ground where the games and celebrations took place.*

Right: *Three of the teams in a six way Tug o' War! Six separate teams picked up the ropes. A central upright fountain was turned on as each took the strain, the aim being to direct the fountain over your opponents. Children attached to each team were issued with large syringes, see in the foreground, filled with water and encouraged to direct them at the opposition.*

Above: *Onlookers at the Jubilee Games, June 2002. Left to right: Mary Wheddon, ?, ?, Norman Nankivell, Paul Cockburn-Mercer, Shirley Cockburn-Mercer, Catherine Meadowcroft, Joan Jeeves, Jane Ball, Mary Willans, Dave Willians, Margaret French, David French.*

Above: *Steam threshing in the 1920s. The figure at the right of the picture is thought to be Harry Reep of Gnattor, and the fifth from the right may be William F. Dodd; the others have not been identified.*

Left: *Wedding party? This remarkable picture of some 14 ladies with just four men apparently dressed for a wedding was taken at Burnshall, Cudlipptown at the end of the nineteenth century. It cannot have been long after James Cole built the house on his return from America. Those seen here have not been identified.*

LIST OF SUBSCRIBERS

Nick and Michelle Abel, Higher Godsworthy
Cottage, Peter Tavy, Devon
Eileen and Cyril Abel, Collaton, Devon
Colin and Victoria Abel, Lower Godsworthy,
Peter Tavy, Devon
Mr R. Abel, Harmony, Manor Road, Tavistock,
Devon
Philip and Alison Abel, Higher Godsworthy,
Peter Tavy, Devon
June Arscott, Fairhayes, Peter Tavy, Devon
Penelope Baker
A.E. Ballard, Longbetter and Will Farms
The Balm family, Wisdom, Peter Tavy, Devon
Daryl and Charlotte Barnes, Horgen,
Nr Zurich, Switzerland
Peter and Anne Barnes, Collymoor House,
Peter Tavy, Devon
Bill and Enid Bellamy, Peter Tavy, Devon
Mr A.J. Berry, Horrabridge, Devon
Ewart and Margaret Blowey, Mount Tavy,
Tavistock, Devon
John and Louise Blowey, Kingford, Tavistock,
Devon
Kenneth S.J. Bod
William Henry Bowhay, Ivy Cottage, Peter
Tavy 1939-1963
John Bowhay, Peter Tavy, Devon
Rosemary J. Briody, Hale, Cheshire
Jane and Richard Burden, Peter Tavy, Devon
K.J. Burrow, Bucks Cross, Devon
Henry F. Carr, Tavistock, Devon
Stephen H. Carr, Tavistock, Devon
Steve and Alison Carreck
Patrick Cashell, Peter Tavy, Devon
Hilary Charleston (née Shepherd), formerly of
Tavistock, Devon
Ann Clinnick
Mrs Ruth Cole, Chaddlehanger, Tavistock,
Devon
Ann Cole, Chaddlehanger, Tavistock, Devon
Mrs Anne Collins, Higher Mill, Peter Tavy,
Devon

Margaret Cook, Tavistock, Devon
Peter Cox OBE and Bobbie Cox, Cudlipptown,
Devon
Douglas A. Craig, Peter Tavy, Devon
Dr Wyn Cudlip, Gomshall, Surrey
Mrs M. Cummings, Tavistock, Devon
Dartmoor National Park Authority
Mr Michael and Dr Helen Day, Nr Loddiswell,
Devon
Mr D.A.R. and Mrs G.M. Day, Worplesdon,
Surrey
Vera and Alan Dean, Harford Bridge Park,
Peter Tavy, Devon/Wimborne, Dorset
W. Dingle, The Bungalow, Moorshop,
Tavistock, Devon
P. Dodd, Chubb Leigh, Peter Tavy, Devon
P. Dodd, Eaglescliffe, Stockton on Tees
Nathan J.W. Dodd, Peter Tavy, Devon
Emily R. Dodd, Peter Tavy, Devon
David E. and Anna L. Dodd, Peter Tavy,
Devon
Sandra and Edward Dodd, Chubb Farm,
Peter Tavy, Devon
I. Dodd, Chubb Leigh, Peter Tavy, Devon
Mrs Judy Drake, Sowtontown, Peter Tavy,
Devon
Eileen Duncan
Hilary Edwards, Bath
Caroline Elmes, Peter Tavy, Devon
Mr R.W. Evans, Boscombe, Dorset
Ian C. Ford, Emerald, Australia
Mr and Mrs Forsman, Dunningwell, Cumbria
Mr Alfred Friend, Coryton, Okehampton,
Devon
P.K. and J. Garland, Horndon, Devon
Lorna and June Gibbings, Streatham, London
Paul Glanville, Tavistock, Devon
George and Rae Glover, South Australia
Ian Gray
Judith Gray (née Brown)
Kathleen Haine, Cudlipptown, Devon
K. Hainsworth, Peter Tavy, Devon

Miss Halliday, Plymouth, Devon
Glen M. Hannigan, Tavistock, Devon
Graham and Katherine Heard, Brousentor,
    Peter Tavy, Devon
Mr Peter, Mrs Julia and Rosanna Henry,
    Youlditch Farm, Peter Tavy, Devon
Mr and Mrs Frank and Daryl Henry, Twyford,
    Hampshire
Lenore Hicks, Tavistock, Devon
George H. Hill, Kingsett, Mary Tavy, Devon
Mrs Valerie Hill and Mrs Rosemary Steer,
    formerly of Langsford Farm, Peter Tavy,
    Devon
Eric and Keturah Hole, Mary Tavy, Devon
Denis Hutchings, Tavistock, Devon
Dr Peter Jackman, Peter Tavy, Devon
Joan Jeeves, Peter Tavy, Devon
Mark G. Jeffery, Tavistock, Devon
Henry Wm Keitch, Peter Tavy, Devon
Colin C. Kilvington, Stoke, Plymouth, Devon
Christina Kimmel, The Hague, The
    Netherlands
Miss Millie Laing-Tate, Wapsworthy, Devon
Bill and Noreen Lane, Peter Tavy, Devon
Angela Larcombe, Peter Tavy, Devon
Martha M. Lethbridge (née Mudge), Tavistock,
    Devon
Loveday Lovell (née Hole), Tavistock, Devon
George and Mina Lowson, Zoar, Horndon,
    Devon
Eleanor Macnamara (Fuge), Australia
Thornton W.E. Madge, Barking, Essex
Douglas Marsh, Mary Tavy, Devon
Douglas Marsh, Peter Tavy, Devon
James and Jayne Medland
Gary and Paula Metters, Peter Tavy, Devon
Mr Huw and Mrs Carolyn Meyrick,
    Hazlemere, Buckinghamshire
M. Millin, Willetton, W. Australia
Jerry and Jill Morris, Hannah, Katy and Abby
    Parsons, Midhurst Cottage
John L. Moses, Tavistock, Devon
Mrs W.J. Mudge, Tavistock, Devon
Claire Nail, Lower Mill, Peter Tavy, Devon
George A. Neale, Loughton, Essex
Mr and Mrs Peter and Olivia Needham,
    Bishop Stortford, Hertfordshire
Barry J. Northcott, Higher North Beer,
    Launceston, Cornwall
Mr N.J. Osborne, Westbury, Wiltshire
Mr and Mrs K.G. Owen, Tavistock, Devon
Jon W. Parfitt, Wilminstone, Tavistock, Devon

Pauline, Harriet and Frankie, Lane End,
    Peter Tavy, Devon
Geoff and Barbara Perry, Whitchurch, Devon
Mr and Mrs P.M. Perry, Plymouth, Devon
John and Mary R. Phillpotts, Cudlipptown,
    Peter Tavy, Devon
Janet B. Piper, Tavistock, Devon
Dennis J. Pratt, Tavistock, Devon
Audrey Prizeman, Plymouth, Devon
Mr and Mrs D.W. Puttick, Eastbourne,
    East Sussex
Mr M. Ralph, Peter Tavy, Devon
Eileen Reid (née Sillick), Peter Tavy, Devon
The Restells, Peter Tavy, Devon
Michael Rice, Australia
Ken Rickard, Lydford, Devon
Mr and Mrs Rolfe, Tamerton Foliot, Plymouth,
    Devon
Mr and Mrs Rolfe, Lower Dimson, Cornwall
Mrs Jenny Sanders, Tavistock, Devon
Peter Saunders, Ringwood, Hampshire
Gerry and Jacqueline Searle, Peter Tavy, Devon
S. and M. Sherrell, Bere Alston, Devon
Dawn Sherrell, Peter Tavy, Devon
Randolph and Kathleen Simmons (née
    Roskilly), formerly of Langsford Farm, Peter
    Tavy, Devon
Doctor J.C. Speller, Tavistock, Devon
Richard T. Staniland, Horndon, Devon
Christine E.J. Stanley, Weybridge, Surrey
Bill Stephens, Leeds
Dorothy Thomas (née Sillick), Peter Tavy,
    Devon
Graham Thorne, Maldon, Essex
Mr G. Waldron, Plymouth, Devon
Richard and Hazel Walker, Coombe Cottages,
    Peter Tavy, Devon
John F.W. Walling, Newton Abbot, Devon
Glazys E. Ware, Exeter, Devon
Sue, Brendan, Nicholas, and Joe Way, Higher
    Churchtown Farm, Peter Tavy
Stirling Way, formerly of Peter Tavy
Rob Weeks, Preston, Lancashire
M. Wheddon, Peter Tavy, Devon
J.A. Whiffin, Oak Cottage
Joyce D. Whiffin, Oak Cottage
Mr P.D. Whitcomb, Salisbury, Wiltshire
A. White, Sunrise, Horrabridge, Devon
Dr H.N. White and family, Wedlake,
    Peter Tavy, Devon
Mrs B. Williams, Tavistock, Devon
Harry and Norah Williams

Titles from the Series

The Book of Addiscombe • Various
The Book of Addiscombe, Vol. II • Various
The Book of Bampton • Caroline Seward
The Book of Barnstaple • Avril Stone
Book of Bickington • Stuart Hands
Blandford Forum: A Millennium Portrait • Various
The Book of Bridestowe • R. Cann
The Book of Brixham • Frank Pearce
The Book of Buckland Monachorum & Yelverton • Hemery
The Book of Carshalton • Stella Wilks
The Parish Book of Cerne Abbas • Vale & Vale
The Book of Chagford • Ian Rice
The Book of Chittlehamholt with
Warkleigh & Satterleigh • Richard Lethbridge
The Book of Chittlehampton • Various
The Book of Colney Heath • Bryan Lilley
The Book of Constantine • Moore & Trethowan
The Book of Cornwood & Lutton • Various
The Book of Creech St Michael • June Small
The Book of Cullompton • Various
The Book of Dawlish • Frank Pearce
The Book of Dulverton, Brushford,
Bury & Exebridge • Various
The Book of Dunster • Hilary Binding
The Ellacombe Book • Sydney R. Langmead
The Book of Exmouth • W.H. Pascoe
The Book of Grampound with Creed • Bane & Oliver
The Book of Hayling Island & Langstone • Rogers
The Book of Helston • Jenkin with Carter
The Book of Hemyock • Clist & Dracott
The Book of Hethersett • Various
The Book of High Bickington • Avril Stone
The Book of Ilsington • Dick Wills
The Book of Lamerton • Ann Cole & Friends
Lanner, A Cornish Mining Parish • Scharron Schwartz &
Roger Parker
The Book of Leigh & Bransford • Various
The Book of Litcham with Lexham & Mileham • Various
The Book of Loddiswell • Various
The Book of Lulworth • Rodney Legg
The Book of Lustleigh • Joe Crowdy
The Book of Manaton • Various
The Book of Markyate • Various
The Book of Mawnan • Various
The Book of Meavy • Pauline Hemery
The Book of Minehead with Alcombe • Binding & Stevens
The Book of Morchard Bishop • Jeff Kingaby
The Book of Newdigate • John Callcut
The Book of Northlew with Ashbury • Various
The Book of North Newton • Robins & Robins
The Book of North Tawton • Various
The Book of Okehampton • Radford & Radford
The Book of Paignton • Frank Pearce
The Book of Penge, Anerley & Crystal Palace • Various
The Book of Peter Tavy with Cudlipptown• Various
The Book of Pimperne • Jean Coull
The Book of Plymtree • Tony Eames
The Book of Porlock • Denis Corner
Postbridge – The Heart of Dartmoor • Reg Bellamy
The Book of Priddy • Various
The Book of Rattery • Various
The Book of Silverton • Various

The Book of South Molton • Various
The Book of South Stoke • Various
South Tawton & South Zeal with Sticklepath • Radfords
The Book of Sparkwell with Hemerdon & Lee Mill • Pam James
The Book of Staverton • Pete Lavis
The Book of Stithians • Various
The Book of Studland • Rodney Legg
The Book of Swanage • Rodney Legg
The Book of Torbay • Frank Pearce
Uncle Tom Cobley & All: Widecombe-in-the-Moor • Stephen
Woods
The Book of Watchet • Compiled by David Banks
The Book of West Huntspill • Various
Widecombe-in-the-Moor • Stephen Woods
The Book of Williton • Michael Williams
Woodbury: The Twentieth Century Revisited • Roger Stokes
The Book of Woolmer Green • Various

Forthcoming

The Book of Bakewell • Various
The Book of Barnstaple, Vol. II • Avril Stone
The Book of Brampford • Various
The Book of Breage & Gurmoe • Stephen Polglase
The Book of the Bedwyns • Various
The Book of Bideford • Peter Christie
The Book of Bridport • Rodney Legg
The Book of Buckfastleigh • Sandra Coleman
The Book of Carharrack • Various
The Book of Castleton • Geoff Hill
The Book of Edale • Gordon Miller
The Book of Kingskerswell • Various
The Book of Lostwithiel • Barbara Frasier
The Book of Lydford • Barbara Weeks
The Book of Lyme Regis • Rodney Legg
The Book of Nether Stowey • Various
The Book of Nynehead • Various
The Book of Princetown • Dr Gardner-Thorpe
The Book of St Day • Various
The Book of Sampford Courtenay
with Honeychurch • Stephanie Pouya
The Book of Sculthorpe • Garry Windeler
The Book of Sherborne • Rodney Legg
The Book of Southbourne • Rodney Legg
The Book of Tavistock • Gerry Woodcock
The Book of Thorley • Various
The Book of Tiverton • Mike Sampson
The Book of West Lavington • Various
The Book of Witheridge • Various
The Book of Withycombe • Chris Boyles

For details of any of the above titles or if you are
interested in writing your own history, please contact:
Commissioning Editor Community Histories, Halsgrove
House, Lower Moor Way, Tiverton Business Park,
Tiverton, Devon EX16 6SS, England;
email: naomic@halsgrove.com

In order to include as many historic photographs as
possible in this volume, a printed index is not included.
However, the Community History Series is indexed by
Genuki. For further information and indexes to
volumes in the series, please visit:
http://www.cs.ncl.uk/genuki/DEV/indexingproject.html